ERROR AND LOSS
A LICENCE TO ENCHANTMENT

© 2018 Kommode Verlag Zürich

Text: Ashley Curtis
Proofreader: Christine O'Neill
Cover Illustration: Patric Sandri
Typesetting and Layout: Anneka Beatty

ISBN: 978-3-9524626-9-0

ERROR AND LOSS
A LICENCE TO ENCHANTMENT

by Ashley Curtis

Kommode
Verlag

But our lot crawls between dry ribs
To keep our metaphysics warm.
— T.S. Eliot, *Whispers of Immortality*

Contents

Preface

This book is written out of the conviction that most of us, by virtue of living in the time we do, suffer under a default world-view whose basic assumptions are so deeply buried in us that we are not even minimally aware of them. Furthermore, these assumptions radically distinguish the intellectual and spiritual life of our time from that of previous eras.

In order to unearth these assumptions and show up their error, it is necessary to dig deep. The tool used for this must, of necessity, be the tool of our time — of our default world-view. This necessitates a delicate balancing act, one in which materialistic science is used to overthrow scientific materialism, in which reason leads us in march-step to the brink of the formless and incoherent. It is my hope that this balancing act can succeed; I find in our time no other way to arrive at a place which, in other times, was the place of origin.

The individual ideas in this book are not original but have been developed and plumbed for centuries and, in some cases, millennia by thinkers far more talented than I. Their combination in this form, however, I have not seen elsewhere, and it is my hope that this may be of some value. I have refrained in general from stating the original sources of ideas by now well in the public domain in the hope of keeping this book less cumbersome and pedantic than it would be if loaded with references and footnotes. When

I have borrowed an idea from a contemporary writer, however, I have noted this.

I will often refer to Darwinism, though without differentiating between the different strands of thought that go by this name or a slightly modified version of it (e.g. neo-Darwinism), nor have I delved into the controversies still raging between evolutionary biologists and philosophers of biology over exactly which strand is most coherent. For me it is enough that natural selection be seen as an indifferent, purposeless algorithm that favours the development and retention of those characteristics of organisms that promote reproductive advantage in the environment in which they find themselves, and that it be understood as the vehicle which produces the 'designs' found in the natural world. It seems to me that any view that goes by the name of Darwinism must see natural selection in this manner and so I believe I am justified in using the term in this rather undifferentiated way.

Ashley Curtis
May 2018

Introduction

It is a commonplace that we live today in a disenchanted world, a world devoid of mystery and magic, a world in which meaning is our own creation, something that we invent rather than discover. Without mystery, without a meaning 'out there' for us to discover, our sense of wonder atrophies. We either go about our pointless existence due to inertia or a remnant of the instinct to survive or else, courageously, we forge a point for ourselves, we create value—in relationships, in creative projects, in pleasure, in work, in the struggle for justice or the search for beauty. Or perhaps we merely revel in the absurdity and freedom of a meaningless existence.

Some writers suggest that our sense of wonder has not disappeared at all but has merely taken up a new abode. Douglas Hofstadter puts it as follows:

> [There are those who] have an instinctive horror of any 'explaining away' of the soul. I don't know why certain people have this horror while others, like me, find in reductionism the ultimate religion. Perhaps my lifelong training in physics and science in general has given me a deep awe at seeing how the most substantial and familiar of objects or experiences fades away, as one approaches the infinitely small scale, into an eerily insubstantial

ether, a myriad of ephemeral swirling vortices of nearly incomprehensible mathematical activity. This in me evokes a cosmic awe. To me, reductionism doesn't 'explain away'; rather, it adds mystery. [1]

Lorraine Daston [2], in a similar vein, suggests that our sense of wonder has moved from phenomena themselves to how we have come to explain them — wonder at such a varied world emerging from so few parts, wonder at the power of the human mind to solve mysteries so convincingly and elegantly, wonder at the explanations themselves — wonder, for example, at a blind and meaningless algorithm (natural selection) 'designing' such a plethora of life forms, including one that creates its own meaning and value. Einstein expresses wonder when he exclaims, 'The most incomprehensible thing about the universe is that it is comprehensible.' And when we think things through we may recognise that, beneath all the hard-wrung explanations of the natural sciences, there still lurk ultimate, unanswered questions — *Why is there something rather than nothing?* — questions that probably lead all of us to wonder from time to time.

We may also wonder at our own creations, be they artistic or technological. A sense of awe at a brilliant musical performance or a painting or a poem that takes our breath away is a kind of wonder. And we wonder, certainly, at moonshots, at 3-D printing, and at the array of miracles our latest smart phones can perform.

---

1   From Douglas Hofstadter, *Reductionism and Religion*, in *Behavioural and Brain Sciences*, 3, 1980.
2   Lorraine Daston. (2014)'Wonder and the Ends of Inquiry', in *Examined Life, Point Magazine*. Retrieved from https://thepointmag.com/2014/examined-life/wonder-ends-inquiry.

Such a surviving sense of wonder would seem to argue for a residual, perhaps essential, 'enchantment' persisting in our world. But these are examples of what one might call a 'meta-wonder'—a wonder directed not at natural phenomena but at our own understanding or manipulation of them, or at the conditions we have discovered for their existence.

And while the conditions of existence, or existence itself, or the things we ourselves have brought into existence, all often do command such a sense of meta-wonder, *actual natural phenomena* are often *dead* for us in a way that for most of our ancestors they were not. There is something missing—we have *lost* something along the way.

Even the most impressive natural displays—lightning, a solar eclipse—have faded for us. We shoot them a glance, to be sure, but generally while going about our business at the same time. Lightning is no longer terrifying—unless we are on a mountain ridge—and it is usually not paid much attention, either. A display goes on outside that puts any fireworks to shame; the sky is ripped apart with streaks and sheets of otherworldly light; horrific crashes shake the ground we stand on—and yet it is all, as it were, *optional*. Watching a solar eclipse at a school last winter, I could not but be struck by the lack of attention it was paid. People milled about outside—some glancing here and there through special lenses at the disappearing sun—and talked and played basketball and told jokes and socialised *while the sun was being blotted out of the sky!* I thought, yes, that's it: the *eclipse is optional*.

It is possible to see this loss as a positive development. Wondering at mystery reveals a lack of knowledge or understanding. Understanding is good: with its attainment we not only gain control and power but also a kind of wisdom, a knowing that is of great use. We are enlightened about the phenomenon in question, no longer 'living in the dark ages'. A call for a return to wonder, from this perspective, is a call for a return to ignorance. The 'deadening' of understood phenomena is not really a loss at all—rather, it is an awakening from delusion to reality. Whatever 'aliveness' lodged in the phenomenon previously was but the result of a misperception—it was a *faux* aliveness, its loss therefore only a pseudo-loss.

The assumption behind this outlook is, of course, that our understanding is both coherent and sufficiently complete to truly dispel the mystery that once adhered to the phenomenon. This book will take issue with both of these claims. It readily accepts the explanations and predictions of our materialistic natural sciences but rejects as both incoherent and incomplete the claims of the world-view I will call scientific materialism—the world-view that I take to be the default world-view of our age, by which I mean the world-view we *really* hold when we are not thinking about world-views.

Chapter One describes in more detail what I mean by scientific materialism and what I mean by a default world-view. For the purposes of this introduction, I will only point out that scientific materialism, in contrast to materialistic science, represents a philosophy and a cosmology, a view of 'how things really are'—a metaphysics rather than a physics.

The confusion of materialistic science, which is both a method (select, predict, test, measure, build model, retest, correct model etc.) and a body of knowledge (in the form of provisional physical and/or mathematical models for selected aspects of phenomena), with scientific materialism, which is a world-view making ultimate pronouncements about what does and does not exist, is so thoroughgoing that it is very difficult to disentangle. One of the goals of this book is to do so. But I wish, also, to go further. I will argue not only that the claims of materialistic science and scientific materialism are completely different but also that while materialistic science *works*, scientific materialism is incoherent. Further, this incoherence is actually *predicted* by materialistic science. Specifically, I will argue that materialistic science sheds a damning light on an assumption so deeply embedded not only in scientific materialism but in almost *all* of our thinking that it does not appear to us *to be an assumption at all*.

Once this assumption has been outed, what kind of world-view can be left to us? If materialistic science gets it right and at the same time scientific materialism is incoherent, what kind of 'world-view' is even possible? And how does this impact the 'disenchantment' of natural phenomena? These are the questions to which this book will offer a response.

Chapter 1

SCIENTIFIC MATERIALISM

A blanker whiteness of benighted snow
With no expression, nothing to express.
— Robert Frost, *Desert Places*

By scientific materialism I understand any conception of the cosmos as an indifferent, value-free physical reality that can exist, and has existed, independently of any consciousness. This cosmos is described increasingly accurately by models of the physical sciences which currently see it as composed, at its most basic level, of particles interacting in space-time via a small number of fundamental forces. These forces and particles have, in the course of vast amounts of time, given rise to circumstances in which life, including conscious and human life, has emerged and developed via a purposeless algorithm (natural selection) that, at base, involves nothing more than the particles moving and reacting as prescribed by fundamental forces. Scientific materialism accordingly sees the cosmos as devoid of any meaning or value except that which conscious living creatures (most notably ourselves) create for it and sees the very tendency to create meaning or value as itself a result of the neutral algorithm which has produced us and our consciousnesses out of inert matter. [3]

This brief precis has, of course, left out almost all of the details of the materialistic science that scientific materialism purports to represent. This is because scientific materialism is *not* materialistic science but a statement on a meta-level *about* materialistic science. It says that, whatever the details of the current version of materialistic science are (and these will change as we come closer and closer to the complete truth, a 'Theory of Everything'), materialistic science can, or will, give a complete description of the universe in the sense that *everything*, from love to lightning, muons to music, religion to racing cars and creation to consciousness, may ultimately be derived from nothing more than the interactions of particles in an indifferent, independent, meaningless universe. It does not claim that the social sciences or studies in the humanities or economic theory are invalid; nor does it claim that the most fruitful explanation for rush-hour traffic is to be found by looking at the quarks and leptons in the drivers and the cars. It does, however, claim that whatever the relevant level of explanation, it is hierarchically reducible to a next lower one, and so on, all the way down to the quarks. Meaning, value, beauty, consciousness, life—none of these require any more 'ingredients' for their making than basic particles interacting according to basic forces, and basic particles and basic forces are indifferent, value-free and in themselves meaningless.

3   Just as I will not differentiate between various strands of Darwinism as long as they agree on the role of natural selection described in the Preface, I will also not distinguish between the various versions of physicalism that I am generally dubbing scientific materialism. While there are salient differences, for example, between eliminative and non-eliminative physicalism, their shared assumption of the mind-independent 'existence' of a material world and their shared belief in a material basis for all entities taken as 'real' qualify both as scientific materialism. For the purposes of my argument, they can thus be treated as one despite their strong disagreements on issues beyond this more general level of consensus.

Error and Loss

These are very strong statements that are to be found nowhere in materialistic science. Materialistic science does not *make* these kinds of statements; instead it creates physical and/or mathematical models with which to explain and predict phenomena. These models are sometimes physical and visible — as with, say, the workings of the solar system; sometimes physical and invisible, as with the model of an electric current as the flow of electrons within conductors; sometimes they are neither, as with the mathematical models of quantum mechanics or in theories requiring fabrics of more than three dimensions. With these latter the 'explanation' side comes up a bit short perhaps — I cannot 'picture' what is happening — but at least the mathematical models provide a means for getting from certain initial conditions to certain verifiable results (including probabilistic results).

Materialistic science is, by definition, materialistic — that is, it explains and predicts phenomena on the basis of models ultimately composed of particles and physical forces. It makes no claim, however, to completeness. It does not claim that it does, will or can explain *everything*. It is, in fact, profoundly uninterested in hypotheses that are not testable by its methods. Is the universe in itself value-free? Does consciousness continue after death? Is the Bach Chaconne in itself beautiful? Does God exist? Science has *no opinion* on these matters because science is in the business of *testing hypotheses empirically* and none of the hypotheses just mentioned can be tested empirically.

Scientific materialism, on the other hand, *is* interested. It holds that God does not exist, that the universe is in itself value-free, that the Bach Chaconne is beautiful insofar as human beings find it so but no further and that consciousness does not continue after death. One could give an endless list of such questions in which science has no interest but to which scientific materialism provides strong answers.

Materialistic science is in the business of testing hypotheses empirically—by doing so, it has arrived at a great number of models that are successful at explaining and predicting a wide variety of phenomena in terms that ultimately can be reduced to the interaction of particles via fundamental forces. Scientific materialism, on the other hand, is a world-view that makes a great number of claims about untestable hypotheses. In particular, it claims that materialistic science tells, or will tell, the whole story.

It is ironic that scientific materialism, which makes the kind of claim that science *never* would, has put over the fiction that it rests on the laurels of science. Science works so well, it claims, that scientific materialism must be the only valid world-view, the picture of the ultimate reality. How has this confusion come about?

One answer lies in a caricature of intellectual history that is widely held to be valid. According to this caricature, religion at one point claimed to know a whole plethora of 'truths' that turned out to be testable by the methods of science. As the results of one of these tests after the other came out contrary to the tenets of religion, a war developed between 'science' and 'religion'—and science kept winning the battles (the geocentric solar system, the age of the earth, the origin of species, etc.). [4]

The results of this caricature are surprisingly far-reaching. Since religion represents a world-view and since science, according to the caricature, defeated (and keeps defeating) religion in battle after battle, it seems only reasonable that science must also represent a world-view—and, further, the victorious one. That science explicitly and carefully does not represent a world-view—that this is, indeed, precisely the reason for its extraordinary success—easily

---

4   For a more nuanced reading of the 'war', see Karen Armstrong. *The Case for God.* New York: Vintage, 2010, Part Two; see also, Nietzsche, *The Gay Science*, Book 1, Section 37.

gets lost in the apparent logic that world-views must do battle with world-views. Scientific materialism, eliding its differences with science proper, now smoothly slips into the gap and claims victory.

A second reason that scientific materialism is in the ascendant today, however, is psychological and far more powerful. It has to do with the ubiquity of technology. While scientific and technological developments are different in kind and the process leading from a scientific discovery to a technological innovation is complex and often accidental, we all realise that in most cases, the technology would not exist without the science—there would be no moonshot without an understanding of gravity, no smart phone without quantum mechanics, no hydrogen bomb without particle physics. Each piece of technology that we see or use or that somehow affects us, from televisions and cars to bombs and toasters—and our twenty-first century lives almost without exception are saturated with such objects—each one proclaims to us, by its very functioning, that *science has got it right*. The leap from 'science has got it right' to 'science presents the correct world-view' is extremely difficult to resist. And again, since science does not *have* a world-view, scientific materialism slides in easily, disguising itself as the inevitable world-view of a science that gets things right.

Exposure to technology is at this point almost global, crossing all lines of class, religious belief and education level. This exposure has an unavoidable psychological effect; it says that someone, somewhere, has got things figured out. When religious, shamanistic or animistic beliefs coexist with exposure to technology, a dissonance, conscious or not, is guaranteed. Successful technology *means* something; it is not a neutral fact to be laid down next to traditional beliefs but is a challenge to them—often consciously unacknowledged, to be sure, but a challenge nonetheless. The fact that technology *works* with a consistency far exceeding that of any comparable traditional practices is inevitably lodged somewhere in the mind. And whether quarks and gauge bosons mean anything—and they likely don't—to the kid lusting after the smart phone, she is, in most cases, perfectly aware that it is 'Western' science that lies behind its construction, and that this science has carefully excised from its discourse anything to do with spiritual or animistic beliefs.

To what extent scientific materialism can be said to be the default world-view that lies unacknowledged behind the professed world-views of various religious or indigenous peoples is, of course, difficult to gauge. Wherever it has not yet established itself, however, it is on its way. On some level *we believe in that on which we rely*—and it is a rare person, today, who does not rely on advanced technology at all. And unless the belief in what we rely on is properly *placed*—as this book attempts to do—the clash of professed with default world-views will not be healthy.

The confusion which merges the successes of materialistic science with the credibility of scientific materialism does not in itself mean, of course, that scientific materialism is wrong. It only means that this sleight-of-hand justification of scientific materialism does not hold water. In the next chapter I will present a number of the standard arguments which have been used to challenge scientific materialism. I do so with the caveat, however, that while we may temporarily be convinced by one or more of these objections, I do not think that this momentary conviction will have any lasting effect on our default world-view. This is because the sleight-of-hand move 'successful science, therefore successful scientific materialism' works at a very deep level within our psyches. The technological onslaught is overwhelming, and it will take something equally overwhelming, something more than a few coherent philosophical objections, to dethrone scientific materialism from ruling over our minds. I will present this 'something' in chapters 4, 5 and 6. There we will see, as I have already suggested, that it is materialistic science itself which leads us directly to the Achilles' heel of scientific materialism.

Chapter 2

FOUR OBJECTIONS TO SCIENTIFIC MATERIALISM

You had such a vision of the street
As the street hardly understands
— T.S. Eliot, *Preludes*

1. Consciousness

Particles of matter interacting according to attractive or repulsive forces would seem to be able to give a convincing explanation for stars, planets, rocks, nuclear and chemical reactions—in short, for physical phenomena. Consciousness, however, seems incommensurate with simple physical being. Consciousness consists of perception, emotions, feelings of pain or pleasure—all of those qualities which make it different to be me rather than, say, a rock—which make it pointless, in fact, to talk about what it is *like* to be a rock and yet coherent to talk about what it is *like* to be me. [5] The possibility of experiencing something as a subject is of a different order of reality than that of being a 'thing' which merely exists. Even if, as no doubt we could if we had enough

---

5 See Thomas Nagel (1974). 'What Is It Like to Be a Bat?'. *The Philosophical Review*. 83 (4): 435–450. For what it is like to be a rock, however, see David Abram, *The Spell of the Sensuous*. New York: Vintage, 1997.

information, we were to assign a physical brain state to each possible qualitative experience of a subject so that, as in the movie *The Matrix*, we could produce any given experience using purely physical means, this still would not even begin to close the gap between the physical and the experiential.[6]

This first objection claims that experience — not the *causes* of experience, i.e. the physical brain-state, but the subjective state of consciousness — is precisely *the* non-physical, and its existence can hardly be explained, rather than correlated, by a physics.

A materialist will reply that we are here naively privileging consciousness. We object to consciousness emerging from a brain state while we are silent about other kinds of emerging: as when a solid, continuous table emerges from the mostly empty space of the atomic lattice that makes it up (the preponderance of material particles in a table being approximately equivalent to that of three mosquitoes in a cathedral); or when table salt, an edible white solid, emerges from a metal (sodium) reacting with a poisonous, greenish gas (chlorine); or when photosynthesis produces solid sugars out of sunlight, a gas and a liquid; or when a clear direction of time emerges on the macro-scale from completely time-reversable interactions of particles on the micro-scale.[7]

---

6   The beginnings of modern science in fact involved precisely the removal of the subjectively experienced from the phenomena under study, in order to observe and measure physical occurrences objectively and without reference to any influence by the state of mind of the observer. Consciousness, being nothing *but* the state of mind of an observer, is that which was intentionally removed in order to get at the physical. Now the physical comes round by the back door to explain that which was removed to get at the physical. There may be a problem here.

7   If we were to see a movie of a man smoking a pipe, say, played once forwards and once backwards, it would immediately be apparent which was which. Forwards would be when the smoke puffs out of the pipe and disperses; backwards when it converges into the pipe and disappears. On this scale time has a clearly recognisable direction. Yet if we were to view a movie of the same event zoomed in so that we saw the individual particles of matter, we would not be able to tell which way the movie was playing.

    The mechanical laws of physics are time-reversible — they work in either direction. Forwards or backwards in time, momentum is conserved, force

          Error and Loss

The critic of materialism is unmoved. For her it is one thing when physical causes produce physical consequences — this is materialistic. The mental is not physical, not material, and it is ludicrous to claim to have derived lived experience from the movement of physical stuff.

2. Values (Beauty, Meaning) Realism

The purely materialist version of the cosmos cannot be complete for those people for whom values (e.g. it is wrong to cause unnecessary harm, or even, it is bad to randomly torture innocent children) are real, indisputable truths, truths independent of whether we believe in them or not. According to such thought, an ethical truth cannot be reduced to a material phenomenon. The materialist view maintains against this that ethical values are evolutionary developments which have promoted reproductive advantage, if not at the level of the organism or the community, then at the level of the gene.

It is important to note that in general scientific materialists do not hold that values, being contingent on a purposeless algorithm

equals mass times acceleration, and so on. The movie run backwards breaks no mechanical laws of physics, only a statistical, that is, a probabilistic one. The Second Law of Thermodynamics defines the forward direction of time as the direction into increasing entropy or, loosely speaking, increasing disorganisation. It works because there are so many more possible disorganised states for a given system than organised ones that, if left to random processes (i.e. nobody is doing any organising), the chance that a system would move from relative disorganisation (dispersed smoke) in the direction of relative organisation (concentrated smoke) is infinitesmal.

Just as a clear direction of time on a macro-scale emerges out of a micro-world in which both directions are completely equivalent, so, one might argue, does consciousness arise from processes that are themselves completely free of consciousness.

in a purposeless universe, are by that token illusory. They do not suggest with Ivan Karamazov that if there is no God, everything is permitted. On the contrary, most scientific materialists hold their secular values dear, and often believe that it is values *derived from religion* that tend to cause cruelty and suffering — from the Crusades to the Inquisition to the witch hunts to terrorism and the mistreatment of women. The values of scientific materialists tend not to have a fanatical tint to them, and the suggestion that they are 'better' values, perhaps for recognising their more humble origins, is not easy to dismiss.

Scientific materialists find mystifying the horror some people feel at the idea of an intrinsically value-free universe in which we create our own values. Why would the universe care if small children were tortured?, they ask. *How* could it care? It is *we* who should care, and we do! Our values, they suggest, are in no way weakened or relativised by being *ours*.

Yet there is room to wonder whether this scientific materialist view is not slightly disingenuous. The Darwinian account of the source of altruism may be cogent, yet what scientific materialist truly bases her idea that young children should not be tortured on this source? Is there not *some* notion of the good at the foundation of materialist ethics? And though this notion may be derived from the workings of an indifferent algorithm, is that what materialists truly *believe* in as its source? The suspicion lurks that the materialists' real source of good is in fact *borrowed* from somewhere other than the materialist creed — where it could hardly be at home. If the notion of the dignity of human beings was first derived from their being made in the image of God, and the notion then gained currency to such an extent that even with the disappearance of God it *seemed* the natural thing to think, and one then thinks it, naturally, without any reference to God, what is the source

Error and Loss

of one's idea? This may, of course, only imply that the materialists are playing a double game and not that materialism itself is incoherent, but it does throw a possible spanner into the works. [8]

The same kind of objection can be made using the idea of beauty or of meaning. Is the Bach *Chaconne* more than *subjectively* beautiful? Has it brushed a reality, an independent essence of beauty, that exists in some way in the universe? Or is it merely very pleasing to the sensibilities of a certain kind of creature (us) by making the particles in us jiggle just so? If the former, then the universe is something more than merely material; it is composed of other essences than matter. Is *Hamlet* meaningful in any objective sense? Or is it merely the case that creatures of our ilk find meaning in it? Scientific materialism, in both cases, opts for the latter interpretation—again, however, with the protest that this does not dissolve meaning or beauty but only locates it exactly where one would expect: in the consciousness of human beings. Nevertheless, if you are what is termed 'a values (or beauty or meaning) realist', this may seem illegitimate to you.

3. *The Ultimate Why*

While materialistic science may currently present us with six quarks, six leptons, their twelve antiparticles, four families of gauge bosons and a set of fundamental constants, it is capable of 'explanation' only down to this level. That is, it explains a huge variety of diverse phenomena in terms of a very limited number of more basic pieces. The explanation for these basic pieces, however,

---

8   This argument is developed at length by Charles Taylor in *Sources of the Self*. Cambridge: Cambridge University Press, 1992.

is simply, 'That's the way it is' — no explanation at all. At an even deeper level, it is difficult to conceive of a materialistic science giving an answer to the question, 'Why is there something rather than nothing?' Even the idea of a kind of natural selection of universes that might be hurled out of some vortex and of which only the fittest survive — those with the right fundamental constants, the right stuff — rather than implode or disintegrate or dissolve, presupposes the existence of *something*, and it seems legitimate to ask, Why anything at all? Why not blank, nothing, nil? (Whether this is actually a coherent question is an issue to which we will return later.) At the foundation of materialistic science, then, lies an unfathomable, inexplicable mystery. When scientific materialism then claims that all existence is explainable by a purely materialistic science, it seems pure hyperbole. And if it wants to exempt this one fact (that there is something rather than nothing) as inexplicable by *any* kind of knowledge and claim merely to cover all the rest, it has drastically weakened its claim to be a complete world-view — not only weakened it but thrown it completely overboard. If I can explain everything except the most fundamental mystery of all, this 'except' so dwarfs all my explanations that they become rather paltry. Is it not, perhaps, to cover just this 'except' that the idea of God has remained in our language? The mystery about which one can say nothing: is not this precisely the *via negativa* of theology?

4. Objective Truth

Scientific materialism would have us believe that just as there are no objective values, there are no objective truths. Truths are ideas that human beings hold to be true; but the universe itself, outside of human thought, does not harbour 'truths'. Truths are our creation.

The question naturally arises as to what kind of 'truth' the world-view of scientific materialism represents. Is it merely a human idea, akin to the idea that small children should not be tortured — valuable in itself, but hardly an objective fact about the universe? Or is it an objective truth about the cosmos, true whether human beings believe it or not, true regardless of whether human beings or any other thinking creatures exist at all?

If the former, it is a rather weaker vessel than it purports to be; if the latter, it is a blatant exercise in self-contradiction.

Here, then, are the four objections.[9] I believe all of them have a certain cogency, but they strike me as attacking the symptoms rather than the root of the problem. They show that something is doubtful somewhere, but do not show what it stems from. In chapters 4, 5 and 6 I will strike at the root of the problem. First, however, I will examine the connection between scientific materalism and loss.

---

9   I have left out what is perhaps the most common objection, that of the proponents of Intelligent Design, because I believe it is based on a profound misunderstanding of natural selection as an essentially random process. For a critique of this view, see Richard Dawkins, *The Blind Watchmaker*. New York: W. W. Norton & Company, 1986.

Chapter 3

LOSS

But how did we do this? How could we drink up the sea?
Who gave us the sponge to wipe away the entire horizon?
— Nietzsche, *The Gay Science*

In prehistoric, animistic times, a stone, a tree, a bolt of lightning
were pregnant with meaning because they were viewed as in some
sense alive. It is difficult for us moderns to imagine what living in
such a world would have been like, a world with mysterious, often
sinister forces and powers intrinsically adhering to material things.

One result of such awareness was a greatly heightened attention and an ability to *see*. Our ancestors paid attention to details
that we blithely ignore because these details had significance,
unknown or guessed at or precisely believed in, and it was worth
paying heed. This was, perhaps, an over-enchanted, but surely
not a disenchanted world. We moderns have not only gained by
abandoning animism—we have also lost. We go through life
without paying attention to our natural surroundings, and our
experience is less vital and less intense as a result.

That we yearn for a world of significant objects is readily

seen in the popularity of fantasy novels, many of which involve objects of power (rings, Horcruxes, moonstones, etc.) and in many of which both animals and plants have special meanings. We create our own special objects — wedding rings, tournament trophies, first dollars earned, etc. — which we treat as having deep significance. New Age shops with their crystals and dream catchers testify as well to our nostalgia for magical items. The common feeling of being alienated from the world is largely a feeling that the *things* in the world are dead, devoid of significance.

When religion replaced animism, the meaning of objects became more indirect but was still there. The bolt of lightning, not itself alive, expressed the anger of a god who was; the tree or stone, as a god's creation, was endowed with goodness (or evil) and thus significance. With the death of God and the ascendancy of scientific materialism, this meaning has been lost. [10] The indifferent, neutral universe contains indifferent, neutral rocks and trees; in the best case, we accept that *we* endow these natural objects with meaning and try to get by with the idea that this is just as good, or perhaps even better — more courageous, more real.

When I step out of a cinema after watching a film, I am often struck by how alive and bursting with significance everything around me appears. The cars in the parking lot, the bushes, the people walking by — all seem part of an intense, larger, highly meaningful picture. I explain this by noting that in the movie such things *did* have significance — every element in the film contributed to its construction of meaning. Of course, these elements were *chosen* by the director or set designer to do exactly this. The movie is, in

10   I take the death of God to refer, not to a general absence of professed belief in a deity, but to the enervation of that deity, its relegation to that corner of life deemed 'religious'.

this sense, a return to a form of animism — a vision of the world in which meaning attaches to objects. This sense of a heightened world lingers for a time outside the cinema, and I have the feeling that this is a richer, deeper, more satisfying way to see things. A short time later, that feeling is gone.

But I have also noticed what is, in a sense, a contrasting phenomenon. When I am away from civilisation for an extended period of time, surrounded not by technological wonders but only by the natural world, my feeling for the significance of objects *grows* with time. I notice more, yes, and what I notice also seems *significant*, much in the way that the cars in the parking lot outside the cinema seemed, for a short time, significant. Animals, stones, water, trees, stars: the longer I am completely removed from civilisation and its attendant technologies, the deeper this significance grows — significance of a kind that I could not express in exact terms but which I feel profoundly. The world begins to become enchanted in a way that I recognise from fantasy novels and what I imagine of our ancestors' animistic past.

The feeling is arresting. I do not seek it — or at least, when I seek it, it does not come. It always surprises. A turn of the head and it is suddenly there, full-on. The rocks are silent centuries of Gregorian chant; the trees are naked spirits; the path, bejewelled, a stairway to heaven, a stairway *in* heaven, and I am walking on decorated air; the world folds, calls, rescinds, opens wide and dissolves; the rivers multiply existences. These are not metaphors, not what things are *like* — they are day visitors, fissures, secret knowledge. They do not explain themselves — they come and go — but there is nothing to explain: the meaning is transparent but unspeakable, investing everything. The longer I am away, the more deeply and consistently it unfolds.

The scientific materialist in me says that the significance I feel sparking and evolving in the objects around me is a significance that I am lending them. The objects themselves consist merely of indifferent matter in indifferent motion in an indifferent, meaningless universe. This is not *bad*, the materialist in me exclaims. The meaning I feel *is* meaning, *real* meaning, as real as meaning can be, just as my belief that one should not torture young children is a *real* ethical belief. That the 'realities' are in both cases created by me, that I am investing situations neutral in themselves with meanings and values that *I* invent should not depreciate the meanings at all. That's the only kind of meaning we have—let us treasure it!

I listen and try to comprehend. And yet ... and yet. I still feel a loss. The world—and I in it—feel diminished. The mystery that I feel *in the objects*—isn't there. They have all been explained. Even my sense of mysterious meaning in them has been explained. And I cannot but think that the mysterious meaning has been explained *away*. It is gone. Lost.

Except it isn't. The mystery is more powerful than the materialism; the unspeakable knowledge drowns the explanation; the clarity of unknowing laughs away the materialist credo. Oh, I believe—*when I'm in it*.

But can I hold on to this? For I must come back down, for food, for company. And as soon as I enter the world so saturated by materialist success—the trains, the cameras, the phones—something shifts. The magic fades. There is too much evidence around me that another way of thinking than the one I have been immersed in *works*, has got it right. I am cudgelled loose from the transparent, unknowing meaning that has filled me.

And I wonder, is there another way to look at it all, a way to avoid this cudgelling? A way, a world-view, a *background* to experience *consistent with the successes* of materialistic science that

Error and Loss

yet cuts the loss I can't but feel that scientific materialism is pre-scribing, hovering as it is in the background of all our electronics and mechanics? One that would remove the power of our gadgets and devices to diminish my felt experience?

Could there be a way that is not delusional wish-fulfilment? A way that would show up scientific materialism *on its own terms*, since it will not admit of others? Could the loss I have been describing be due, not to an unwelcome but undeniable reality, but to an unseen *error* at the very foundation of the scientific materialist world-view? I believe that it is, and in the next three chapters will attempt to root out and explicate this error.

Chapter 4

ERROR (I)

You sober people who feel armed against passion and phantastical conceptions and would like to make your emptiness a matter of pride and an ornament—you call yourselves realists and insinuate that the world really is the way it appears to you: before you alone reality stands unveiled, and you yourselves are perhaps the best part of it—oh, you beloved images of Sais! But aren't you too in your unveiled condition still most passionate and dark creatures, compared to fish, and still all too similar to an artist in love? And what is 'reality' to an artist in love! You still carry around the valuations of things that originate in the passions and loves of former centuries! Your sobriety still contains a secret and inextirpable drunkenness! Your love of 'reality', for example—oh, that is an old, ancient 'love'! in every experience, in every sense impression there is a piece of this old love; and some fantasy, some prejudice, some irrationality, some ignorance, some fear, and whatever else, has worked on and contributed to it. That mountain over there! That cloud over there! What is 'real' about that? Subtract just once the phantasm and the whole human *contribution* from it, you sober ones! Yes, if you could do *that*! If you could forget your background, your past,

your nursery school — all your humanity and animality!
There is no 'reality' for us — and not for you either, you
sober ones — we are not nearly as strange to one another
as you think, and perhaps our good will to transcend
drunkenness is just as respectable as your belief that you
are altogether *incapable* of drunkenness.
— Nietzsche, *The Gay Science*

In this chapter I will attempt to locate the fundamental error that
I see both in the philosophy of scientific materialism *and* in the
criticisms levelled against it. I believe that this will allow us to *place*
materialistic science and its successes in such a way that a broader
ultimate perspective emerges than that of scientific materialism,
one capable of withstanding the daily assaults that Airbuses and
smart phones rain down on the other critiques.

According to the neo-Darwinian branch of our materialistic
science, the reasoning abilities of *Homo sapiens* will have developed
as an evolutionary adaptation to serve reproductive advantage. Just
as ethical values exist only insofar as we believe in them, and we
believe in them only because it is (or has been in our evolutionary
history) advantageous to the survival of our 'selfish' genes, so our
powers of reason will have developed to promote the survival of
these genes and not to deliver an objective, ultimate 'truth'. And
just as we have been 'designed' to believe in our values (which
don't objectively exist), so we will have been 'designed' to believe
in the results of our reasoning — else it would hardly be to our
advantage.

This *reason*, which allows us to manipulate nature consciously
in a way that no other animal can, depends on a highly developed
language. This language allows us to ask, What if? It allows us
to imagine counterfactual situations. It allows us to quantify and

Error and Loss

measure, to conceive of space as mapped or at least mappable and of time as linear, clocked and calendared. It posits causes in the place of patterns. It allows us to develop a belief in the permanence of objects even when we are not experiencing them.

How did reasoning powers, and the language they depend on, contribute to the survival of *Homo sapiens*? By allowing us to strategise, to foresee the consequences of hypothetical actions and to arrive at explanations of past events which allow us to control future ones. We became able to design and build tools, lay traps, control fire and plan hunts in ways that were no longer instinct-based but deliberate. [11] Our survival behaviour became less 'instinctual' than that of other animals and more 'rational'. In one way of looking at it, this 'reason' separates us from other animals. For materialistic science, however, we *are* other animals. A better way of looking at it would be to say that reason has not replaced instinct, but that reason has *become our chief instinct*.

Our skill set *works*. And here comes a subtle and difficult distinction. Materialistic science tells us that we have these skills because they work, they allow us to manipulate nature in a way that confers reproductive advantage. Bats echolocate because it works; pit vipers see heat because it works; the sense of smell of wolves is so highly developed because it works. Not because it is 'true', not because it leads to knowledge of an objective reality, but simply because it works. Our reasoning, contrary to what we tend to believe, falls into this same category.

Our reason, along with the language and conceptualisations that support it, has developed to allow us to gain reproductive advantage by consciously manipulating the world we experience.

11   And these same skills, just like the bone that morphs into a spaceship in Kubrick's film *2001: A Space Odyssey* suggests, are now useful for building Airbuses and smart phones.

There is an evolutionary warrant for believing that they will do this effectively. A faulty instinct doesn't work; it leads to extinction, not success. But there is *no* evolutionary warrant for believing that this same reason is any good at all for creating world-views which are irrelevant to survival. [12]

This view of reason as an instinct, as our chief survival mechanism, as that which confers on us reproductive advantage, goes against deeply engrained beliefs. We tend to think that reason is a generally valid tool, somehow self-evidently so, and *among* its uses are such as favour our survival. This idea of reason as so transparently truth-delivering that it needs no justification runs from Plato to Augustine and all the way to Daniel Dennett and Thomas Nagel. And yet, just as Darwinism sees no warrant for hypothesising objective values that our ethical sense leads us to, so it cannot see a warrant for hypothesising objective (as opposed to useful) truths to which our reason leads us. Instead, both our values and our reason are pitched towards optimising the likelihood of the survival of our selfish genes.

Yet the jump from 'it works' to 'it is true' is so engrained in us that it is very difficult to remove. What we have always done, as metaphysicians, no matter what the metaphysics, is to assume that a language, a reason, a set of concepts that was indifferently yet brilliantly 'designed' to manipulate nature would also be useful for describing what is ultimately real.

I will call our reasoning ability 'niche-reason', indicating

12   This point is made by Thomas Nagel in *Mind and Cosmos, Why the Materialist Neo-Darwinian Conception of Nature is Almost Certainly False*. Oxford: Oxford University Press, 2012,. but he runs the other way with it. Since for him reason is transparently valid as a general truth-discerning mechanism, Nagel supposes there must be something wrong or at least incomplete in Darwinism. My suggestion is that Darwinism is fine, and the problem lies in the idea that our reason is generally valid.

both that it forms our evolutionary niche and that it is designed to be applicable in this mode and not otherwise. And because this idea, of our reason fitting an evolutionary niche rather than being a generally applicable truth-delivering mechanism, is so foreign to us, we will turn in the next chapter to a parable which lays out an example of exactly how this is so: The First Parable of the Beech Tree.

Chapter 5

ERROR (II)

To be without a description of to be.
— Wallace Stevens, *The Latest Freed Man*

The First Parable of the Beech Tree

I go into the woods in early summer and see a beech tree.
I see that it has smooth, grey bark and a tangle of
branches, that its green leaves are surrounded by soft
downy hair. I touch the beech and feel the grainy texture
of its trunk; I pluck a leaf, tear it in half, and smell,
then taste it. Then I return home, ten kilometres away.
From here I cannot even see the forest.

As I drift off to sleep I remember the place where the
beech tree was—a white rock below it, a steep slope,
patches of fresh grass in the leaf mould, a deer track cut-
ting just above it. I remember the beech tree, calling
to mind a grey, smooth-barked, green-leaved image, and I
murmur, 'The beech tree is there.'

Let us look at my experience of the beech tree. What I see — smooth, grey bark; moist, peaked leaves; twisted branches — is, I believe, something outside of me. I realise that my experience may be different from that of someone who has no interest in trees and doesn't know it is a beech, who sees a rather less differentiated tree; or from that of a botanist, who surely sees far more than I do in the tree. It is certainly a different experience from the one an alien would have, especially an alien who has never before seen or heard of trees. Yet all four of us would agree that the tree exists independently of us — that is to say, if we were not looking at it, the same tree would still be there. Our language allows us to express this belief succinctly: 'The beech tree is there.' We even believe that, were all conscious life in the universe to be suddenly snuffed out, the tree would *still* be there.

Surprisingly, there is something profoundly incoherent, almost meaningless, about this common-sense view. The view is so engrained in us, and our language handles the situation so effortlessly, that the incoherence is difficult to see, but let's make an attempt. Let us ask what we *mean* by the statement, 'The tree is there,' independent of anyone's experience of the tree. When we say it 'is there' we picture it — meaning we call to mind our experience of it (grey, smooth-barked, leafy etc.) and imagine the tree — by which we mean a grey, smooth-barked, leafy thing — standing in the place in which we saw it.

This move is incoherent. It is incoherent because what I am calling to mind when I think 'The beech tree is there' is not the tree *independent of my experience*, but precisely *my experience of the tree*. Grey, green, smooth, of a certain shape and size — all the attributes I think of as belonging to the 'tree' are actually attributes of my experience of the tree.

This is easy to see when we reflect that 'grey' and 'green' have no meaning to a person blind from birth, who could never think of the tree as grey and green. Smooth would have no meaning to a person with no sense of touch. What such people would mean by 'the tree' would *not* be a grey, green, smooth thing, because these terms would be meaningless to them. Meanwhile, if someone were to be gifted with the vision of a hawk, 'The tree is there' would mean something different again — the kind of image that we, with three receptor-sensitivities in our eyes, cannot have, but the hawk-person, with four, could. What we think 'is there' when we say 'The tree is there' is thus clearly bound up with our experience of the tree.

Without vision or sense of touch, not only colour and texture but size and shape are meaningless. Shape is an entirely visual concept, one not shared by the blind, and our idea of size is overwhelmingly visual as well. As we shall discuss shortly, the blind, who can feel objects, do not think of them as having size in the same way at all that sighted people do. Thinking of the tree *apart from experience* as having size or shape, then, also makes no sense, as size and shape are also only aspects of *experience*.

We are trying to make sense of the tree *apart from* experience, apart from *anyone's* experience. What is this completely experience-independent 'tree'? It is now tempting to say it is an object that *would give rise* to a grey, smooth, green, large *experience* if a being who could perceive colour and texture were to encounter it. It would give rise to grey and green, for example, by reflecting electromagnetic waves of certain frequencies into their eyes; it would give rise to size and shape by filling a certain height and breadth with the atoms that reflect this light and also resist touch. Thus, one might say it is an object that emits such and such waves and exerts such and such resistive force when touched from such and such positions.

This would seem to settle the matter. And my hunch is that this is how most of us think of it. But it won't do at all.

All we have done, by this reasoning, has been to transfer the onus of 'being' from the 'tree' which we experience as grey, green, of a certain shape and size to an *object which would give rise to the experience* of grey, green and a certain shape and size. But what do we mean by 'object' here? Can we conceive of an 'object' except *as* a thing with size, shape, colour, texture etc.? Try it—you will see that you cannot do it. And so, the incoherence has merely jumped from the experience-independent tree to the experience-independent 'object'.

We take words which describe attributes of our experience—grey, large, twisted—subtract the experience and imagine that the words still have a meaning. But if colour, shape and size already would have no meaning to a consciousness without vision or a sense of touch, then *how could they have meaning in the absence of any consciousness at all?* And it is precisely this, the tree in the absence of *any experience at all*, that we are trying to get at.

I am not quarrelling with the logical move, with the *reasoning* moving us to 'an object that would give rise to a grey and green experience if a colour-perceiver were to pass by'. The logical move is perfect. The conditional language employed by the logic functions brilliantly, along with the (exclusively) human notion of causality, which dictates that an effect (our experience) must have a cause (the 'object that would …'). This is just what our niche-reason prescribes.

My point is a different one. My point is that the logic coherently employed by our niche-reason leads to a statement whose *content* is incoherent. 'An object which would give rise to a grey and green experience if a colour-perceiver were to pass by' is an attempt to describe an object *apart from experience*. How does it

Error and Loss

do this? Purely in terms of an *experience*! We have not come any closer to the *unexperienced* 'object'.

We might consider other attributes of the tree, though, such as its mass. Can this, perhaps, give us the hold we are looking for on the unexperienced tree? Let us subject mass to a similar analysis. When we say the tree has a certain mass, we mean something by it. We mean that it would put up a certain resistance to acceleration or, alternatively, that it would balance a certain quantity of standard masses on a scale. Both of these 'woulds', however, again depict experiences. They imagine us applying a certain net force to the tree and measuring its acceleration (or simply, qualitatively, pushing it in a frictionless environment and feeling the resistance) or placing it on a balance scale which we level by placing standard masses on the other side (or simply, qualitatively, trying to pick it up). Without such imagined experiences, the concept of mass has no meaning. Without any imagined experience, 'five kilogrammes', for example, is just empty notation.

The attribute of mass is less directly available to us than those of colour or shape and so the experience involved is at a further remove. We could be fooled about the tree's mass more easily than about its shape — for example, by a cleverly painted Styrofoam dummy of the tree. The experience of mass is not, as with shape, 'I see the outline', but is rather the thought, 'I bet if I cut it down and tried to lift it, it would be damned hard.' The meaning of 'mass', however, is just as based on experience, in this case the experience of imagining the resistance put up against a push or the resistance to lifting against gravity. Mass also, then, is a concept that requires experience — in this case an imaginative experience — in order to have meaning.

A further attempt to get around the problem of coherently describing the unexperienced beech tree would be to say it is a collection of such and such atoms (or quarks and leptons) bound together in such and such a way. Again, however, the onus of being has simply been displaced — this time not to a single 'object', but to a collection of many 'objects' bound together. But whether we are talking about one 'object' or many 'objects', the problem is the same. It doesn't matter how many 'objects' we are talking about if we can't make sense of what an 'object' means devoid of all experience. Just as the unexperienced beech tree is described as an 'object that would give rise to a perception if a perceiving being were there', so the unexperienced quark can only be described as an 'object that would give rise to certain measurements if a measuring being were there'. Measuring is an experience as much as perceiving — it is nothing more than perceiving the behaviour of an instrument. In both cases, then, something which is supposed to be outside of experience is described purely in terms of an experience.

We cannot talk coherently about *anything* outside of all experience because we need experience to give us the language *with which* to talk about it. Even the most abstract things — say, non-Euclidian geometries, or spaces of ten dimensions — rely on our experience of thinking about them, our experience of calculating, notating, representing, following logics. *Ideas, too, are experiences.* Would non-Euclidean geometry 'exist' if there were no one anywhere to think about it? The answer is neither yes nor no. The question is instead incoherent, and for exactly the same reason that the question of whether the beech tree 'exists' in the absence of all experience is incoherent: namely, the concept 'exist outside of all experience' is nonsense. We can't know what it means because it would require us to know something outside of our experience — and since knowing is itself an experience, it cannot reach outside of experience!

Error and Loss

If this idea seems tautological, that's because it is. We cannot get beyond our experience because any experience we have 'outside of our experience' becomes itself part of our experience. And even every thought is an experience. The tautology is not trite only because we consistently and stubbornly ignore it, because we regularly insist on the coherence of talking about what 'exists' completely outside of our experience.

Let us make one last, desperate attempt to circumvent the tautology. I am again going to leave behind the beech tree, but this time I will put an instrument in place which measures the electromagnetic waves reflected by the atoms that make up the tree and sends the results of its measurements to a remote location. I will then go to the remote location, see that the instrument is measuring light of the frequency that gives rise in me to the experience of the colour green and say, 'Hah, you see! The beech tree is there and it is green.'

What is happening here is that I am experiencing the beech tree at one remove via the instrument. Instead of seeing it directly with my eyes, I am 'seeing' it indirectly with a measurement. Instead of having a 'green' experience, I am having, say, a 560 Terahertz experience (that is, an experience of reading a display that says '560 THz'). Moreover, I am experiencing the idea that the beech tree (which I picture as grey, green, twisted, etc.) is emitting the radiation being read and displayed by the instrument.

There is a *lot* of experiencing going on here. One could try to parcel it out and define which part of it is experience of the instrument, which of the display, which of the information, which of the idea of the tree and so on, but we will not do this. We will not do this because our point is precisely that we can try to make such sense of things here only because there *is* experience—lots of it—while the problem that bedevils us is: What is the beech tree without *any* experience? If consciousness had not developed in the universe, if there were no sentient beings, no awareness of anything at all, what would a beech tree be then?

When we propose to talk about the beech tree *in the absence of all experience, all consciousness*, we are setting ourselves an impossible task, precisely because *we are conscious*. As soon as we imagine something, consciousness is there—and consciousness is precisely that which is required to be absent.

When we posit the 'existence' of a beech tree outside of all experience, we are attempting the impossible. We are making an *ontologically meaningless statement*.

'Ontological' is a fancy word for 'having to do with "being", with "existence"'. 'The beech tree is there' is an ontologically meaningless statement because we cannot know what 'existence' means in the absence of experience, as we cannot know what anything means in the absence of experience.

Given the fact that 'The beech tree is there' in the absence of any experience of the tree is an *ontologically meaningless* statement, it is perhaps surprising that 'The beech tree is there'—still in the absence of any experience of the tree—is at the same time undoubtedly an *experientially useful* statement. It is, in fact, extremely useful. If I need firewood for the future, it is *useful* to know that the beech tree is there and I could go make firewood of it. If I want to meet you at a certain time, knowing that the beech tree is there is very *useful*, as I could suggest that we meet at the beech tree and we would thus find each other. Darwinism suggests that our language/reason is *useful* precisely in such ways. It claims, however, that statements about 'being' in a philosophical rather than a practical, utilitarian sense have no evolutionary warrant to be seen as meaningful. And, as we are now seeing, Darwinism is here perfectly correct.

Error and Loss

How can 'The beech tree is there' (in the absence of any experience of the tree) be a *useful* statement if it is ontologically meaningless? Very easily. While it has the *form* of an ontological statement, it actually functions as a *code* for a completely different statement, an *experiential* statement. It is a code that we all understand perfectly well—and the encoded experiential statement has a perfectly clear meaning. 'The beech tree is there' *does not mean* 'The beech tree is there'. It is instead a coded way of saying, 'If you move in such and such a way, you will experience the beech tree.'

This eminently useful statement is a statement about *experience*, rather than about *being*. It tells me that if I take a certain action, I will have a certain experience. This is a coherent statement. I know what it means, because *I know what it is to experience*.

My claim that 'The beech tree is there' is *meaningless* as a statement about the existence of the beech tree does not imply that it is *wrong*—i.e. that its negation ('The beech tree is *not* there') is correct. Not at all. My claim is another: it is that both statements are meaningless, just as 'the gaftry is floobaloo' is neither a correct nor an incorrect but a meaningless statement.

Thus, I am in no way saying that the only thing that exists is our experience, or even *my* experience. To claim that 'reality' is my hallucination, for example, that nothing exists outside of my consciousness, would be to make an equally meaningless statement: namely, the statement that the beech tree (or the physical world) does not exist. I am instead pointing out that *we don't know what we mean* by 'exist' or 'not exist' in the absence of experience. And if we don't know what we mean, then we are using empty ciphers—no matter whether we use them in a positive or a negative statement. We have come up against our limits. We are incoherent.

Perhaps we ought now to revise our original statement of the problem. We have claimed that 'The tree is there', without all experience, is an ontologically meaningless statement because the separation of being from experience will not hold water. Perhaps a better way of looking at this, however, is that the entire idea of *ontology* is flawed. If ontology is to mean having to do with 'existence', in contradistinction to having to do with experience, then it cannot but be a nonsense concept. Thus, rather than saying that 'The tree is there' is an ontologically meaningless statement, we must make the larger claim that it is a meaningless statement *because it is an ontological statement, and ontological statements can have no meaning*. Ontology is a pseudo-concept. If we can't know what 'exist' or 'not exist' mean in the absence of experience, we can't know what we mean by 'ontology' in the first place.

In order to guard against misinterpretation, I would like to emphasise that two common ideas, which may seem related to the First Parable, are in fact irrelevant to it. The first is the distinction in typical discussions of scientific realism between objects which we can perceive directly with our senses and those we cannot. A beech tree falls into the first class; a quark into the second. The exposition of the First Parable does not distinguish between the incoherence of unexperienced quarks and that of unexperienced beech trees. That quarks are not experienced directly through our senses, but indirectly as ideas abstracted from measurements made by instruments, makes no difference to the import of the parable.

The second idea is that of the 'inference to the best explanation'. This idea suggests that, if our experiments with quarks work so well, if models based on quarks are such excellent predictors of observable phenomena, then the best explanation of this concordance is not that there's some cosmic joke or coincidence that

Error and Loss

makes the quark models so effective, but that quarks are *really there*. Quarks, then, are more than pieces of a model that successfully predicts phenomena; they are actually 'real things', and their being 'real things' is the most likely reason for the model's successful predictions.

This idea operates on a completely different level from the First Parable. It is addressing the question, are quarks 'real things', or are they not 'real things'? One or the other alternative is held to be necessarily correct, and the 'inference to the best explanation' suggests that it is the former. The First Parable, however, claims that the whole dichotomy is bogus. 'Real things' (i.e. things that 'exist'), in the absence of all experience, is an incoherent concept. So is 'Not real things'. Rather than taking one side or the other in the debate (in technical terms, the debate between 'scientific realism' and 'instrumentalism'), the First Parable dissolves the debate.

This dissolving of the debate might be labelled a form of 'pragmatism', but even this appellation would be misleading. A 'pragmatist' view would say that, since it can make no conceivable difference to *anything* we experience whether quarks are 'real' or merely useful pieces of a model that predicts well, it makes no sense to discuss the matter. Because it makes absolutely no difference which alternative is correct — no difference to our experience, no difference to our predictions, no difference to anything at all that could conceivably affect us in any way — we a) cannot possibly resolve the issue and b) ought not have any *interest* in resolving the issue. In fact, there is no actual meaning attached to the ideas of 'correct' or 'incorrect' in this context. The debate is over.

This is an honourable argument, but it is *not* the argument of the First Parable. This is why the First Parable is framed in terms of beech trees rather than in terms of quarks. As I have noted,

'The beech tree is there' appears to be an ontological (and therefore meaningless) statement but is actually very meaningful as a coded statement about experience. And whether a beech tree is there or not (read as a code) *does* make a difference to our experience. If it is there and I cycle straight towards it, I will get hurt, whereas if it isn't there, I won't. If it is there, I have firewood; if not, I don't. The First Parable claims that there is no meaning to the 'ontological' statement, 'The beech tree is there', in the absence of any experience of the beech tree, despite the fact that we can — in contrast to the situation with the quarks — perfectly easily verify that the practical statement, 'The beech tree is there' (i.e. if you move in such and such a way, you will see the beech tree) does potentially affect both our predictions and our experience. It is, then, not a pragmatic argument at all.

To summarise, it is important to note that the First Parable is not about scientific realism vs antirealism, that the 'inference to the best explanation' argument is irrelevant to it and that it is not merely a restatement of a pragmatist perspective. It claims rather, in the simplest of terms, that the thought 'The beech tree is there', in the absence of any experience of the beech tree, is an 'ontological' and therefore an incoherent thought, even though practically it may be correct and affect us in all sorts of ways.

We are so used to letting our language have its way — it is so easy to say, 'The tree is there' — and it is so *useful* to do so, that the idea that we might be making an incoherent statement, a statement with no referent, is very difficult to grasp. And yet the situation gets even worse, for we have so far only been concentrating on the 'tree' aspect of 'The tree is there'. What about 'there'? 'There' refers to a location in space. Space, however, is also something we experience. We experience ourselves here, and other things

Error and Loss

over there, and this distinction between here and there forms the basis of our concept of space. But if no one is making this distinction, where is the space? What could we possibly mean by 'there' without experienced space?

This idea is perhaps even more difficult than that of the incoherence of the attribute-less tree. This is because we have a map-oriented concept of space, a concept which appears to us transparently and necessarily correct. We think of space as spread out like a map; even when we ourselves are at the upper left corner of the map, we still carry with us a perspective on the whole map. We imagine the map, say, with a token (us) in the upper left corner and yet believe that the whole thing, including the lower right corner, is 'still there'.

This is not the only possible conception of space. Animals surely do not think of space in terms of a map, though they are generally far better navigators than we are. Conceivably space for certain animals is more like a story — first this happens, then this — or is negotiated as a sequence of smells; or, as with migrating birds, as experiences of magnetic fields. Animals do not have a 'concept' of a 'there' that lies waiting in a corner of the map, but rather, if at all, as a 'there' that lies at the end of a series of actions.

We can, perhaps, imagine an alternative, non-map conception of space if we think of playing a video game in which we steer a character through a landscape. We steer our character, on the screen, through a forest and then down a road past a red house on the right to a stream. We then turn the character 180 degrees and steer her past a red house on the left and back into the forest. We have returned to where we started, but surely do not have the idea that this place was waiting for us, as it would be on a map, as we undertook our journey. Rather, the place (say, a small beech tree with lovers' initials carved into it) was no longer anywhere;

it was recalled by the software when our steering satisfied certain conditions. This might be rather like an animal's 'conception' of space—when a particular smell is followed by another one and then another one again, the doghouse is experienced again.

Perhaps even more revealing of the contingency of a map-like concept of space is the complete lack of it in the blind from birth. People who have been blind from birth and who, later in life, receive sight through medical intervention, lack a map-like conception of space altogether and must learn it from scratch. Marius von Senden reports in his book, *Space and Sight*:

> But even at this stage, after three weeks' experience of
> seeing, 'space' as he conceives it ends with visual
> space, i.e. with colour-patches that happen to bound his
> view. He does not yet have the notion that a larger
> object (a chair) can mask a smaller one (a dog), or that
> the latter can still be present even though it is not directly
> seen. (…) In walking about it also strikes him—or
> can if he pays attention—that he is continuously passing
> in between the colours he sees, that he can go past a
> visual object, that a part of it then steadily disappears
> from view; and that in spite of this, however he twists and
> turns—whether entering the room from the door, for
> example, or returning back to it—he always has a visual
> space in front of him. *Thus he gradually comes to realize*
> *that there is also a space behind him, which he does not*
> *see.* [13] (…) Those who are blind from birth … have no real
> conception of height or distance. A house that is a mile
> away is thought of as nearby, but requiring the taking of a

13   My italics

Error and Loss

lot of steps … the elevator that whizzes him up and down gives no more sense of vertical distance than does the train of horizontal. [14]

This excursus on alternative conceptions or non-conceptions of space is meant to bring home the fact that our map-like conception of space is not the only possible one; in fact, it is an exclusively (sighted) human one, a highly reasoned variety, one learned, invented. With it, we make up for our extremely poor instinctual notion of space. We can't compete with birds or salmon or dogs without the aid of a highly reasoned, mapped-out space—which is okay, because we do quite well with our maps. It is our 'niche-reason' that allows us to set up space like this; it is our language of conditionals and counterfactuals, our 'ontology', that allows us even to conceive of a map in which places that no one is experiencing are still abstractly held to 'exist'. ('The tree *is* there.')

Thus, it is not only *objects* that we cannot conceive of separate from our experience, but *space* as well. What we mean by space is determined by our experience of space, and our experience of space is contingent on who we are (sighted people, blind people, animals …).

In the end we can make the point most effectively, perhaps, exactly as we made the point with the beech tree. What do we mean by space in the absence of any being to experience it? We mean something that *would be experienced as space* if a person (or other conscious, space-perceiving being) *were* to experience it. We are trying to describe *unexperienced space* and the only way we can do it is *in terms of an experience*. We simply can't get there from here.

14   Marius von Senden, *Space and sight: The perception of space and shape in the congenitally blind before and after operation.* London: Methuen, 1960.

From the incoherent notion of a non-experienced space we now return to the idea of a non-experienced 'there'. In our minds, 'there' is also a place that *looks* like something. Our beech tree is next to a large white rock, near a deer trail, on a steep slope, etc. The attributes of 'there' are known to us only as experiences. What could we mean by 'there' without the experience of that place? When we think 'there', we picture it, that is we re-experience it in our imagination. But this is something happening in our imagination — this is a 'there' of the mind. Without this picture, without anyone having *any* picture, what could 'there' possibly mean? What is 'there' without the experience? What is it like? Without any mind, what is a 'there' of the mind? Just like the unexperienced tree, it has no attributes. It is incoherent.

One could attempt to say that by 'there' I mean 'at such and such coordinates on the map'. This, however, is to stand the whole thing on its head. The map, including coordinates, is a representation, an artificial construct, designed to model what we think of as 'space', to make up for our otherwise poor instinctual ability to experience space in other ways. To use the map, which is a derivative of place, to define a place is as it were to use a recipe to taste a meal.

What is the point of this parable? The thesis delineated in the previous chapter claims that our language-based reasoning — our reason-instinct, our niche-reason — would be expected by Darwinian theory to be *useful* — that is, to confer reproductive advantage — rather than lead towards true statements about what is ultimately real. The First Parable of the Beech Tree shows exactly this: our niche-reason is clearly making a useful statement when it says, 'The beech tree is there'. This useful statement would also *seem* to be making a true statement about what is real, in the

Error and Loss

sense that it postulates something we refer to as the independent existence of the beech tree and its correlation with the independent existence of a place called 'there'. This 'true statement about reality', however, reveals itself on close inspection to be not untrue but incoherent—saying nothing while seeming to say something. As an 'ontological' statement, it must, like all 'ontological' statements, be meaningless; translated into the only meaning it can be said to have, it is actually a *useful* statement *about experience*.

This is exactly in line with what our (useful) materialistic science, in its neo-Darwinian garb, predicts. Our 'niche-reason' is, like the instincts of all animals, a survival mechanism, not a truth-discernment mechanism concerning what is 'real'.

It is enlightening to note that materialistic science, in the hands of careful practitioners, intentionally avoids 'ontological' statements (statements about what *'really exists'*) from the ground up. 'Observables' in science are not defined as entities that *exist*, but rather as measurements made by following a specified set of procedures. In the jargon, these 'observables' in science are defined 'operationally':

> All the quantities physicists call 'observables' are operationally defined, that is, they are specified in terms of measurements performed by well-prescribed measuring procedures. Temperature is what we measure with a thermometer. Voltage is what we measure with a voltmeter … Time is operationally defined as what is measured on a clock. [15]

15   Victor J. Stenger, 'Time, Operational Definition of', in *The Encyclopedia of Time*, H. James Birx, ed. Forest Oaks: SAGE Publications, 2009, pp. 1293–1294.

The clock by which time is ultimately operationally defined today happens to live in Colorado:

> … the primary time … standard is now provided by averaging a set of *Cesium Fountain* atomic clocks at the NIST laboratory in Boulder, Colorado, which at this writing will not gain or lose a second in more than 60 million years … All of the observables in physics are now calibrated against the time measured on the standard clock … Specifically, the international standard of length, the meter, is the distance traveled by light in 1/299, 792,458 of a second in a vacuum … So, as it now stands by international agreement, all physics measurements reduce to measurements made on clocks … the process of measuring time involves counting ticks.

It is significant that a careful materialistic science does not conceive of observables as 'things' but as experiences resulting from following specified procedures. There is not a meter—there is instead a procedure for measuring in metres. This is a subtle but essential point. Earlier, I noted that we are not helped out of the incoherence of the unobserved beech tree by collecting measurements made in our absence and suggested that the statement, 'The beech tree is there', only has meaning when interpreted as a code for the statement 'If you move in such and such a way, you will experience the beech tree.' Notice that measurement itself, in a carefully conceived science, is specifically defined as a code: 'The beech tree is thirty-five metres tall' means, 'If you follow the agreed-on procedure for measuring the length of the beech tree, you will come up with a measurement of thirty-five metres.' A careful science recognises the danger of incoherence lurking in

Error and Loss

the idea of 'things' out there. A second is not a 'thing', but if you follow a given procedure, you will arrive at a measurement in seconds that all can agree upon. A quark, an electron — these are, ultimately, ideas used as tools for predicting measurements. Even the most cursory acquaintance with quantum mechanics makes clear that thinking of the electron as a 'thing' is quite impossible.

Dear reader, this First Parable is very difficult and I fear that my exposition has not been clear enough; I fear that you may be frustrated with me and consider my ruminations absurd. The problem is that we are so used to thinking of our reason as a generally valid truth-discerning mechanism and successful scientific reasoning as *one example* of this mechanism of general validity. What I am doing here is standing the paradigm on its head: I am saying, as Darwinism would suggest, that our reasoning is an instinctual behaviour designed *only* for delivering useful, survival-enhancing results (i.e. in the broadest sense, for doing science) and that the *extrapolation* from its use in attaining such results to conceiving of it as a generally valid truth-discerning mechanism is unwarranted. Our problem in seeing this is that we, even as neo-Darwinians, perhaps *especially* as neo-Darwinians, are not Darwinian *enough*! We want our truth, dammit, and for this we are happy to close our eyes to a little inconsistency.

Here an objection may occur to the attentive reader. If our reason and our language are so ill-equipped for general truth-discernment, then this book must itself be incoherent. Or am I as its author claiming a unique ability to sound out the truth that I am denying to all other naturally selected *Homo sapiens*?

My response is as follows: No, I do not claim such an ability, as will be evident in the remainder of this book and as the astute reader may already foresee. The only way I can show up scientific materialism as a world-view, therefore, is by showing, not that it fails to live up to *my* elevated standards (I do not claim to have these), but rather by showing that it fails by its *own* standards. I am not required to know better — in fact, my claim will be not to know at all. But I can still show that what is on offer is unconvincing, because the kind of reasoning *it itself relies* on for its validity will not support it.

Dear reader, even if this First Parable of the Beech Tree seems to you incomprehensible gibberish, I encourage you to read on. The Second Parable of the Beech Tree is significantly easier to grasp, and after we have examined it I will even make an argument specifically designed for those of you who do not buy my exposition of the First. That is to say, this book does not continue on the assumption that I have already convinced you with my exposition of the First Parable; on the contrary, it assumes that many readers will not be convinced (yet!). For these readers, too, there is more in store.

Error and Loss

Chapter 6

ERROR (III)

How do you know but that ev'ry Bird that cuts the
airy way, is an immense world of delight, clos'd by your
senses five?
— William Blake

The Second Parable of the Beech Tree (Part One)

I am experiencing the beech tree, but this time I have been
blind from birth and live in an isolated society of
people all of whom also have been blind from birth. We
experience trees by touching, smelling, hearing, perhaps
tasting them. We have a word for what feels, smells,
sounds and tastes just so: *trees*. Those trees which have a
certain texture, which have a certain smell, whose
leaves taste so and so, we call beech trees. So, I am experiencing what I know to be a beech tree.

There is no sense of sight in our society and moreover,
we have never had contact with any people who can
see. Sight is simply not a concept for us. And the idea that
the experience of a beech tree could be radically other
than ours, the idea that a beech tree could have properties
such as colour, shape, shading, is not even conceivable to

us as we do not know what these are, do not even have a language for them.

The Exposition of the Parable

From a sighted perspective, the people of this society have only a very limited notion of a beech tree. They are missing the sense perception, the concepts and the language to access that huge part of beech-tree-ness that is visual. Neither do they have any way of knowing of their limitation, any way of knowing how incomplete their knowledge of beech trees is. And yet they are able to fell trees, chop wood, make fires to cook and heat.

How could we possibly know that we are not in a similar situation with regard to the 'world' that we experience? Indeed, if one grants, contrary to the First Parable, that it makes sense to talk of a world 'existing' external to and completely independent of our consciousness, the chances that we would happen to be so fitted out, perceptually and conceptually, as to perfectly match, or even approximately match, what is *out there*, are vanishingly small. Even in comparison with animals that we know, our perceptions are laughable. If dogs reflected and considered, they would find us dim-witted with respect to the central constituent of the world, smell; bats would find our ability to echolocate worse than paltry; pit vipers would find our infrared vision pathetic; and hawks, who can see the flapping of bees' wings, the rising of thermals and magnetic fields, would find us all but blind. And these are only the perceptual modes that we in fact *share* with these animals and regarding which we merely compare poorly. Other forms of perception, for which we do not even have a vocabulary, would show us beech trees from a side we never dreamt of.

Error and Loss

The point of this parable, then, is that it is absurd to suppose that our knowledge of a beech tree, or anything else, can ever approach completeness. If the universe truly exists independently of our experience of it, we have absolutely no warrant to suppose that we have either the perceptual or the conceptual apparatus to be able to connect with all of it and no reason to suppose that we connect with more than a tiny portion of it—a portion that includes what is necessary for our survival.

I now wish to use the First and Second Parables to make points that may seem contradictory, and indeed in a sense they are. I am playing devil's advocate for the moment, and this does not bother me for now, though I do hope to achieve a non-contradictory synthesis later.

As I laid out in the previous chapter, I believe that the statement 'The tree exists', absent any experience of the tree, is either a code for a quite different statement or a meaningless bit of nonsense. As I mentioned at the end of that chapter, however, I am not confident that you, dear reader, will see it that way. I think that you may still believe that, even when no one experiences it, the tree is there in a sense more substantive than as a coded 'If I move in such and such a fashion, I will see the tree.' I want to take this seriously, and in two ways. First, it seems to me that your belief in the meaningful 'existence' of a thing that is not experienced by anyone *entails* that you believe the proposition illustrated by the Second Parable: that there are aspects of the tree, perhaps essential aspects, to which we are blind; that this thing, this tree, could only be completely known to us if, in fact, it *did* depend on our experience to exist—that is, if it *were* our experience of it. In this case—if the tree were nothing more than our experience of it—speaking of aspects of the tree beyond our experience would indeed make no sense. But given that you believe in the cogency of its completely independent existence, you must admit that you cannot be sure that we are not missing a sense—or seventeen, or a million senses—or a conception or a language that would make the tree seem completely other than it does to us now, as it would seem completely other to the blind person were she to gain sight. And of such aspects, what they might be like, we cannot even begin to guess. By this I mean that our missing 'sense' might not even be analogous to the senses we possess—could include, for example, experience of something like the *consciousness* of a tree. What more there is, we simply cannot say, not even what kind of thing it might be.

Once you sever the tree completely from our experience of it, then you render it unthinkable that we should actually have complete knowledge of the tree as it 'is', in all its aspects. (Unless, of course, the world was so designed that we, *Homo sapiens*, would have a perceptual and conceptual apparatus that fits perfectly with the independently existing world around us, and there is absolutely no evolutionary warrant to believe this is so. This would require a God, a purposeful designer. And we know in any case from the examples of animals with 'other' or far better developed senses, that our match with what exists is far from perfect, as theirs is in so many respects superior.)

On the other hand, if you *do* accept my argument that the statement 'The tree exists independently of any experience of it' is a meaningless or at best coded statement, then the whole premise of scientific materialism drops away and scientific materialism cannot be correct. The idea of an indifferent, neutral universe that exists independently of any conscious creatures to experience it—the very premise of scientific materialism—can be no more coherent than that of a beech tree that exists independently of our experience. The idea is not right or wrong—it is incoherent, meaningless.

Either way, then, scientific materialism is doomed. Either the universe exists totally independently of us and cannot be known in any way approaching completeness by human beings (including those who espouse scientific materialism), or the universe cannot be meaningfully said to exist independently of us and scientific materialism is demolished from the word go.

But let us not allow scientific materialism to fall without a fight. The argument I have just made may seem airtight, and yet it is still possible to try to circumvent it. It is possible to attempt an end run around the dichotomy I have just presented in order to avoid its conclusion. The end run looks like this:

Let us accept, contrary to my interpretation of the First Parable and consistent with scientific materialism, that it makes sense to talk of a beech tree (or an indifferent universe) 'out there', independent of any consciousness. Then, of course, as the Second Parable suggests, there may be things 'out there' which we as human beings cannot experience. We cannot claim to know such things. But we can try to obtain knowledge of everything that is out there *that will ever be relevant to us.*

A thing 'out there' could, potentially, either affect us or it could not. If it could, then it will likely show up in experiences that we have in some way or other (if not directly, then indirectly through measurements or other effects). Accordingly, it could be accounted for, observed, noted and potentially predicted or explained by materialistic science. If it could not possibly affect us in any way, it is completely irrelevant to us and consequently we should not care about it.

Thus, if materialistic science *à la* the Second Parable is

'missing' large parts of the universe—that is, if scientific materialism is wrong—it doesn't matter in any conceivable way that it is wrong, because we would never experience any ill effects. In fact, we would never experience any effects at all. Only if materialistic science were 'missing' something that could ever matter to us would we feel the effects of this 'missing'. But then the Second Parable would no longer apply. If we ever feel the effects of any wrongness of materialistic science, then we modify the science so that it captures, or predicts, or explains whatever it is that is affecting us. If materialistic science is missing out on some essential feature of human experience, then that's merely because it's not (yet) living up to its own mission, and it can adapt accordingly.

Thus, scientific materialism is entirely cogent. It claims not that materialistic science can explain everything that exists out there independently of experience, but merely everything that could potentially affect us—everything, that is, that it makes any kind of sense to talk about.

Let us note that the end run involves a massive retreat from the original claim of scientific materialism. Materialistic science is no longer said to explain everything but only *those aspects of the cosmos which are relevant to us*, only those aspects *to which we have access*. This retrenchment is a significant weakening of the scientific materialist position. It leaves open the possibility that there are vast aspects of the universe which exist, but which materialistic science cannot access and explain.

But even this retrenchment is suspect for it presents a glaringly contradictory mishmash of assumptions. On the one hand, it claims that it makes sense to talk about what is 'out there', independent of any experience, e.g. the indifferent universe that exists without us; on the other hand, it claims that it makes no sense to talk about anything 'out there' that cannot in any way *affect* our experience.

In attempting to make this end run around the Second Parable, then, this way of thinking runs into conflict with its own interpretation of the First. It is contradictory to maintain *both* that it makes sense to talk about an 'out there' that 'exists' independently of any experience *and* that it makes *no* sense to speak of things 'out there' that cannot in any way affect our experience. In the first case, 'making sense' does not depend on there being experience; in the second case, it does.

Whoa, wait a minute, cries the end run. We are here, we exist and we have certain conceptual and perceptual capabilities. We have access to certain but not all aspects of the universe and can make sense of them. We know what barren rocks are, what swirling conglomerations of gases are, because we have experienced them (at first or second hand). And we can imagine them existing *in our absence*, precisely because we have experienced them *in our presence*. All we need to do is to 'subtract' our consciousness from this experience and we will have it. We *cannot* imagine, on the other hand, those aspects of the universe for which our conceptual and perceptual capabilities are not adequate, since we will never have experienced them. If there are aspects, as the Second Parable suggests, not in our realm, we cannot imagine them at all. But those things in our realm which we *have grasped*, we can imagine existing without us, precisely because we *have* experienced them existing *with* us.

And now we must say thank you to the end run, because it has brought the question to a head. *Can* we imagine things — barren rocks, swirling conglomerations of gases, empty space — existing without us? *Can we 'subtract' ourselves from our experience?*

Let us try. Let us conduct a thought-experiment to find out.

Let us suppose that, as scientific materialism claims is completely plausible, life had *not* developed in our universe. That event which first kicked off self-replicating behaviour in molecules never happened. Barren rocks, gases, stars inhabit the map-like space of the universe, but no life, no consciousness — no *experience*. We can imagine this, right? We can see the bare surfaces of planets, feel the heat of swirling conglomerations of gases, write equations describing the reactions in the nuclear furnaces of the stars. Right? It doesn't need us.

Wrong! This thought-experiment is impossible — impossible, because it relies on *thought*. And thought is exactly what is ruled out by the premises of the experiment. We cannot imagine a universe without any experience in it because, whenever we try to do so, we imagine *our experience* (of swirling heat, of bare surfaces, of space, of the logic of equations). We cannot 'subtract' all consciousness from the experiment because the experiment *can only happen via consciousness*! This is exactly the point of the First Parable.

Despite this obvious fact, this tautology — that I cannot 'subtract' my experience from my experience and expect to have something left over — it still seems to us that we can do it; it still *seems* so *easy* to do. Dear fellow human beings, do you not see how bad we are at this? I, too, think I can do it — to me it is so easy to imagine the universe without conscious beings. I forget, while doing so, that the very *imagining* I am doing requires consciousness. I am so convinced that I can see it, feel it, work it out. And yet this seeing, feeling, working out is exactly what is precluded by a 'reality apart from experience'. This thought-experiment is *completely* incoherent.

We are all trapped in our experience, which includes our concepts, categories, beliefs, imaginings, knowledge — and it is obviously impossible for us to go beyond it. As soon as we do go

Error and Loss

beyond where we have been already, we have added another realm to our experience, rather than stepped outside of it. The unexperienced beech tree makes no more sense than an unexperienced *aspect* of a beech tree. *Neither one is accessible to us.* If you buy the one, you have bought the other. This is why the end run, already a severely weakened form of scientific materialism, does not work.

At a certain point, we come up against our limits. These limits are determined by the fact that, although we would like to imagine a completely unexperienced 'reality', we are incapable of removing experience from what we imagine. Imagining is itself, *entirely*, an experience. We can string the words together easily enough — we can say, 'That which exists, independent of any experience of it' — but the words are empty ciphers, nonsense posing as sense.

Before we examine just where this leaves us and what we are to make of it, there is one more piece of the puzzle which we need to examine. We will do this in the next chapter, with the Third Parable of the Beech Tree.

Chapter 7

UNNATURAL SELECTION

One day I, Chuang Zhou, dreamt I was a butterfly,
fluttering hither and thither. I was conscious only of my
happiness as a butterfly, unaware that I was Zhou.
Soon I awaked, and there I was, veritably myself again.
Now I do not know whether I was then a man dreaming
I was a butterfly, or whether I am now a butterfly,
dreaming I am a man.
— Chuang Tzu

I have argued that the kind of reasoning that we are good at,
which to a large extent forms our evolutionary niche (akin to
a bat's ability to echolocate), is useful but not truth-discerning
and that this is exactly what our materialistic science, in its neo-
Darwinian garb, would lead us to suspect. I have commented on
the overwhelming temptation to suppose that a reason so robust
as to be able to produce Airbuses and smart phones *must* be
generally applicable, applicable also to discovering philosophical
truths, but have suggested that there is no warrant to succumb
to this temptation, and, indeed, that to succumb to it would be
an anti-Darwinian move. But it is probably still mystifying, even
if you accept my argument, *how* such robust reasoning could
simultaneously produce Airbuses and yet fail to speak coherently

of unexperienced beech trees. On the one hand, to be sure, it is our language that tempts us to believe that ontological statements can have a meaning beyond their coded, experiential, useful one. (We have seen that such statements are carefully circumscribed by our physics in its most fastidious form.) There is a further level of explanation, however, that comes strongly into play and may help to de-mystify the *how* of this failure. This is that our reasoning, when used for successful scientific purposes, is directed towards an *already selected* variety of phenomena.

Pure natural sciences examine phenomena that are *objective, repeatable and measurable*—not all phenomena and certainly not 'aspects of the cosmos that are inaccessible to us' (how could it?). [16] No, science looks at objective, repeatable and measurable phenomena and, as might be no great surprise, discovers objective, repeatable and measurable results. A quark is, fundamentally, an abstraction from *measurements* that anybody could make ('*objective*'), *repeatedly.*

This preselection is essential to understanding the apparent conundrum. If I go trick-or-treating and, from among all the candy offered to me, put only Snickers bars in my trick-or-treat bag, and then turn up at home and show my parents, they may find it mind-boggling that the only treat anyone offered that Halloween were Snickers bars. But there is nothing mind-boggling

16   The formulation 'aspects of the cosmos that are not accessible to us' naturally runs against the entire tenor of the First Parable. It is nonsense as it implies that it is meaningful to talk about something 'existing' in the absence of experience. The point here is that even if my exegesis of the First Parable were wrong and it *did* make sense to ascribe meaning to existence without experience as scientific materialism does, such 'existence' would be outside the scope of materialistic science. It is only scientific materialism that claims to have 'everything' in its scope, and since it insists on the meaningfulness of mind-independent 'existence', this either includes 'aspects of the cosmos that are not accessible to us' or, as in the end run, exempts them at a great cost to its own consistency.

Error and Loss

about it. Science likewise appears to have mind-boggling success with everything it touches. But it only touches that with which it can have success.

The Third Parable of the Beech Tree illustrates how this preselection works, and why it is so effective.

The Third Parable of the Beech Tree

A curious investigator wishes to ascertain whether a beech tree that falls in the woods with no sentient being around makes a sound.

The common-sense notion of a sound, she knows, is something that someone, or some being, hears. On this count, it is clear that the tree does not make a sound. A physicist presents her, however, with a different notion of sound. Sound for the physicist is a longitudinal wave of compression and rarefaction in a given medium, in this case air. The physicist points out that this 'sound' is *objective* (doesn't rely on the experience (hearing) of a subjective observer), measurable (by a device that detects the rarefaction and compression and assigns them numerical values) and repeatable (one could allow many trees to fall at different times and check for the same result.)

The physicist suggests to our curious investigator that she set up a rarefaction/compression measuring device that records its results over time in the vicinity of the tree, enclose the forest in a soundproof box, make a cut almost through the tree, set up a remote device to give the tree the necessary extra push, exit and trigger the device. Examining the recording of rarefactions and compressions in the air for the time at which the pushing device was triggered, our curious investigator would be able to discover whether the tree did indeed make a sound.

The Exposition of the Parable

Redefining sound from 'something that is heard' to 'compressions and rarefactions in a medium' is a very clever and useful move. It allows one, apparently, to answer decisively a question that otherwise would seem intractable. It allows one to answer it because one's object of study is now objective, measurable and repeatable.

Notice, however, what it has done to the phenomenon of sound. It has made the question as to whether a sound occurred equally answerable by a hearing person and a completely deaf person. Both can read the detector and conclude: yes, rarefactions and compressions occurred in a medium, therefore, sound.

On the one hand, this is fine and good. It is eminently useful. Looking at sound in this fashion allows one to make sound producing and recording devices, for example. It would even allow deaf people to make sound producing and recording devices. It allows one to predict, unambiguously, that falling objects make sounds. Combined with a little anatomy, this view of sound even *explains* the mechanism by which we hear.

On the other hand, this is absurd. By selecting precisely that aspect of the whole phenomenon that is objective, measurable and repeatable, we have ended up with a 'sound' equally accessible to the deaf and to the hearing. And we have left out a whole host of aspects of the situation that are not objective, measurable and repeatable. We are not asking, 'Does it make sense to talk about an "object" that is not experienced? What do we mean by such an "object"? What does "falling" mean in such a case? Is the "sound" the "tree" makes beautiful?' We are not investigating that sound qualitatively, we are not opening our ears and minds to the richness and subtlety of the sound as a sensation. We are not plumbing the *being* of the sound-sensation as we only can by hearing the sound, by deeply merging with it in the core of *our* being.

Questions and openings of our minds like these are the apples, the Reese's Cups, the Butterfingers that we have not admitted to our trick-or-treat bag. And so, the bag comes home laden with Snickers bars.

Even if we shift the focus of the scientific investigation to such openings of the mind, even if we were to study, with MRIs and questionnaires, the phenomenon of people merging with sound, we would end up only with propositions about what is objective, measurable and repeatable about such merging rather than the merging itself. What is inevitably missing from the propositions (e.g. 'Sound is compressions and rarefactions in a medium', or 'Merging with sound involves an activation of such and such regions of the brain', or 'Sound-merging is most effective after fifteen minutes of mantra-meditation') is the actual experience. And as I will argue in the next chapter, this very experience represents a 'truth' inaccessible to any kind of scientific investigation, a 'truth' that cannot be captured with a proposition.

That human niche-reason — and thus materialistic science — *works* should not be surprising, any more than that echolocation works for bats or infrared vision for vipers. Echolocation and infrared vision, however, are not comprehensive truths about the universe. They are skills *limited* in application — they find bugs and mice. Bats do not echolocate to find lions nor do vipers use infrared vision to locate airplanes. Bugs and mice are the

Snickers in the bags of bats and vipers, just as explanations and predictions of objective, measurable and repeatable phenomena are the Snickers in the bags of human beings.

A bat can echolocate, very well: if it couldn't, it wouldn't be here. Echolocation does not establish truths about ultimate reality, but the bat doesn't care. A pit viper sees heat and a hawk sees thermals, both very well: if they couldn't, they wouldn't be here. But seeing heat and thermals does not establish truths about ultimate reality. Nor do hawks and snakes ask it to do so.

Homo sapiens applies a certain kind of thinking to manipulate the world of our experience; we do it very well, otherwise we of the scrawny physiques, chicken-flavoured flesh and poverty of other instincts would not be here either. Like echolocation and infrared vision, our kind of thinking does not establish truths about ultimate reality either. But for us this *is* a problem, because we *want* it to.

How we could satisfy our lust for such truths without falling into the trap of metaphysics is the subject of the next chapter.

Chapter 8

TRUTHS

Pilate therefore said unto him, Art thou a king then?
Jesus answered, Thou sayest that I am a king. To this end
was I born, and for this cause came I into the world,
that I should bear witness unto the truth. Every one that
is of the truth heareth my voice.
   Pilate saith unto him, What is truth?
— John, *18:37–38*

Where does this leave us? I would like to return to the Parables
of the Beech Tree and look at them in another light.

We are a different kind of animal species from all others
in that our niche is cognitive. This predisposes us to ask the big
questions. My argument has been that this has led to massive
confusion, that our 'niche' concepts and language are not even
remotely adequate for the big questions that they themselves
tempt us to ask — so that not only any answers, but even the
questions themselves, like the idea of the unobserved beech tree,
are incoherent. And this leaves us not in a state of knowledge but
instead standing before mystery.

The Third Parable of the Beech Tree illustrates how I can
come to know, in one sense, what a beech tree is — a plant made
mostly of air (the bulk of its mass comes from atmospheric CO_2), a

photosynthesiser that converts sunlight to sugar, an object of such and such mass and such and such chemical composition—namely by selecting from among the questions I could ask about the beech tree those limited ones which can be answered objectively, repeatedly and with measurement. I know that if I wanted to learn more, a botanist, a biologist, a chemist and a physicist could each give me reams of information at the corresponding levels—arrived at also by limiting the scope of their investigations to these particular kinds of questions. Although in this 'niche' way I know what a beech tree is, the First Parable points out that I can coherently conceive of the beech tree, the object of this scientific knowledge, the thing the scientists are talking *about,* only as my *experience* of the beech tree, largely as something seen and felt; and that the beech tree in the absence of my experience, in the absence of shape, colour, texture etc.—and especially in the absence of *any* experience—makes no sense to me and so remains *mystery.* But the beech tree harbours even more mystery than this, for there is the Second Parable. When I experience the beech tree (that incomprehensible mystery), I am aware that this experience of colour, shape, texture etc. is only what my limited perceptual and conceptual apparatus can handle and, had I other modes of perception and conception, my experience would be far different from what my limitations currently allow. In this sense, too, the beech tree is a mystery, as vision is a mystery to the blind, and especially to those blind who have never heard of seeing.

I am delighted with what materialistic science tells me about the beech tree. I find it fantastical and magical that it is mostly made of air and that it turns sunlight into sugar. I am sure, however, that it is not telling me the whole story—in the face of the mysteries I have just noted, science is exhausted, in the wrong movie—but that is well and good. Science knows what movie it is in and behaves accordingly. When scientific materialism comes along, however, and claims that materialistic science *is* telling the ultimate story, that there is nothing more to it, I cannot but find this claim immensely naive.

And this recognition is wonderfully freeing. Not because I wish to build an alternative philosophy which *will* tell the whole story—hardly, for this would be impossible. As a good neo-Darwinian, I accept that our reason is the result of natural selection for reproductive advantage and is *not* a discerner of ultimate truths. And as the author of the Beech Tree Parables, I recognise that there is no evading the mysteries of the beech tree, nor of anything else, even should I want to.

No, the recognition is freeing because it allows for the possibility that the movement towards scientific explanation and prediction is not a movement that disposes of mystery, *even at the level of the object*. Properly *placed*—first as useful, second as restricted and third as intentionally self-limiting—scientific explanations *complement* mystery, rather than dissolve it. And I am not speaking primarily of the 'Why is there something rather than nothing?' level of mystery that inevitably runs at the foundation of every explanation and which in any case I now consider to be an incoherent question—I am speaking about a mystery attending to phenomena *themselves*, a mystery on the same level as that which got lost when animism and then religion became displaced by scientific materialism. Wonder, awe, terror as a stance towards phenomena—trees, rocks, lions, lightning—is not a stance that a materialistic science discredits or renders illusory and appropriate only for children. Neo-Darwinian materialistic science, by providing us with the expectation that our 'niche-reason' be useful rather than truth-discerning, rather *opens up a place* for wonder of the old, animistic kind.

This wonder, however, is now properly *placed*. Our materialistic science and its derived technology *work* and we know to enhance the fertility of our fields with decomposed organic matter rather than with child sacrifice; our science has led us, as it should, from things (child sacrifice) that don't work to things that do—but in doing so, it has only replaced a non-functional explanation with a functional one. The replacement of a superstitious explanation with a scientific one, however, is on a different level from the replacement of mystery with wonder-cancelling knowledge.

What, then, of the urge to know, the desire for the ultimate truth that our cognitive talents push for? Must I simply be frustrated? Must I sit with hands clasped, shaking my head and saying, I don't know, I can't know?

Yes and no. The word 'know' carries at least two senses. One is, to have discovered a true proposition. I know that George is in the dining room means that I am certain of the truth of the proposition, 'George is in the dining room'. 'We know that electrons repel each other' means we are certain of the truth of the proposition, 'Electrons repel each other'.

Another sense of 'know', however, refers to a deep level of experience. 'He knows cars' does not mean that he is certain of a proposition about cars, but that he 'gets' cars, he is extremely experienced with the way cars are. Biblical 'knowing' refers to two people experiencing each other in an especially intense and intimate way.

My thesis is that although we have been fooled by our niche-thinking into believing that we want to 'know' the truths of the universe, of existence, *propositionally*, in the same way that we know that two isolated masses will accelerate towards each other, in fact this is not what we want at all. Rather I think that

Error and Loss

this 'need to know', properly placed, is a drive for knowledge in the second sense. It is a wish to have a 'true'—deep, intimate, intense—*experience* of the phenomena we encounter. And the misguided search for a cognitive ultimate truth, a final proposition, only takes us further and further *away* from such experience.

The Second Parable of the Beech Tree (Part Two)

One day a sighted person from the outside world comes into contact with our blind society. She describes her experience of the beech tree. It is, of course, unfathomable to the blind, except that they realise she is describing an experience of the beech tree which they have never had. They realise now, cognitively, that the beech tree is infinitely more than they had ever thought it was—it is, however, incomprehensible to them just of what this 'more' consists.

And then one of the blind begins, little by little, to develop the faculty of sight. Little by little, fuzzy and undifferentiated at first, the visual experience of the beech tree becomes accessible to her. [17] It is such a treasure (O brave new world, that has such beeches in it!), so unlike anything she has experienced or been able to imagine, it is such a *revelation* to her, that life becomes a ceaseless delight. Her experience has become richer. She has seen. She wonders.

17   The actual acquisition of sight by the blind is in fact a jarring and confusing process, and a beech tree is certainly not immediately recognised as such—see the discussion in Chapter 4 of blindness and space. I am here assuming and compressing a successful move into the world of the sighted.

And when she has grown accustomed to sight, though she marvels at it always, it occurs to her that the beech tree harbours still other marvels. What other senses, other concepts, other languages might be brought to bear on the beech tree, revealing themselves analogously to the visual revelation for her? For she is now merely in our sighted position and cannot help but wonder, what more, as yet unperceived, might still inhere in this marvellous tree?

The first part of the Second Parable of the Beech Tree made the point that if we grant the independent existence of the beech tree, there must be aspects of it beyond those which we can perceive and of which we can conceive. The 'end run', attempting to rescue scientific materialism, suggested that it makes no sense to talk of such aspects, as they can never affect us in any way. In considering this argument, I showed that it implicitly contradicts the idea that 'independent existence' can have a meaning, taking us back to the First Parable.

With this second part of the Second Parable we are now back with themes raised in the end run. There we assumed that we could draw a neat line between accessible and inaccessible aspects of the beech tree. The second part of the Second Parable suggests that this line may not be so neat. It depicts the line as capable of being breached.

Once it has been breached, the end run would say, it becomes part of experience and thus capable of being catalogued, searched for regularities and tested. Note that if it were breached only once, momentarily, it could neither be searched for regularities nor tested: no science could make anything of this 'seeing', as it never happens again (is not repeatable). And yet despite this

Error and Loss

inaccessibility to science, it would profoundly *affect* the one who has 'seen'. She is aware now of a 'beyond' to which she has had access. The end run fails, then, also on this count: there *can* be experiences that affect us and yet are not susceptible to scientific investigation.

But let us not stop here. For there are other, far less trivial ways in which an extension of perception or conception into the area beyond our ordinary experience might remain inaccessible to scientific investigation.

Scientific knowledge comes about by forming and testing hypotheses. But forming hypotheses to explain or predict is contingent on a certain way of reading the world, a way which sees it as explicable and/or predictable. Our evolutionary niche invites us to read the world in this way — it is how we get by.

Animals do not read the world like this. They do not form hypotheses; they act and react. And although it is difficult for us to imagine, there may be aspects of the world which can *only* be experienced in this way. In such a realm we would also become, cognitively, the equivalent of wolves. The 'normally inaccessible' aspects of the beech tree may represent such realms — realms accessible *only* to non-hypothesising, e.g. wolf-like, experience.

It may be objected that what I am doing here is taking our experience, which extends *past* that of the wolf in that it includes hypotheses and predictions, isolating this 'extra' that we as humans bring to the wolf-experience, and improperly suggesting that we cannot bring it to *whatever* experience we want, including that 'beyond' the beech tree.

This idea that we bring the hypothesis-experience and add it to the wolf-experience to create a human-experience is, however, deeply flawed. This is because we do not *have* the wolf-experience. We don't bring something in addition to it, because we never have it to bring something to. After a very young age human-experience is shaped, at all levels, by hypothesis-experience; it is something *completely* other than wolf-experience. And wolf-experience is also not merely human-experience minus hypothesis-experience. On the one hand, human-experience minus hypothesis-experience makes no sense, and on the other hand, wolf-experience contains so much *more* that human-experience is missing, both perceptually and instinctually. Hypothesis-experience is *one kind of experience*, wolf-experience a completely *other*. They cannot be combined, *as each destroys the other*. To say that an aspect of the beech tree beyond our ordinary experience *must be accessible* to hypothesis-experience, and thus to science, is an illegitimate move. We cannot know to what kind of experience it is accessible. It may only be accessible to wolf-experience. And, of course, I am only using wolf-experience as an *example* of non-hypothesis-experience. The point is not that the aspects of beech tree experience posited as possible by the Second Parable are only accessible to wolves but that they may be accessible only to non-hypothesis kinds of experience.

Hypothesis-experience cannot be brought to every realm. [18] In fact, removing hypothesis-experience *opens up realms*. Rather than being applicable in every realm, hypothesis-experience actually *shuts realms down*, as is testified to consistently and repeatedly by mystics, yogis, psilocybin-eaters, stroke victims, athletes and performers experiencing 'flow' etc.

This shutting down of realms has been accepted more and more as congruent with 'reality', while non-ordinary experiences

---

18   There may be realms, for example, to which clock-time and map-space cannot be applied. Clock-time and map-space, we remember, are human constructions, not givens of the universe; animals, babies, mystics and, in part, the blind do without them. Dreams often ignore or warp them. Without clock-time or map-space, it is difficult even to conceive of what the word 'prediction' might mean.

Error and Loss

have increasingly been shunted aside as quirks and delusions, as scientific materialism has gained more and more explicit or implicit sway in our lives. If scientific materialism provides the ultimate answer to questions about the universe, then it is the hypothesis-experience which is the privileged one and the others are lesser, lacking, illusory. This is why it is so important to recognise that scientific materialism is an incoherent world-view. Hypothesis-experience is not privileged. It represents our survival niche and nothing more.

We have now reached the point at which we can attempt a synthesis of the First and Second Parables, which have seemed, until now, contradictory. The First Parable claims that the idea of a 'reality' independent of all experience is incoherent; the Second Parable, on the contrary, seems to take such a reality as its premise and claims that if it 'exists', then there is no way around the fact that our knowledge is woefully incomplete. The virtue of these parables, taken together, is that they render scientific materialism, *by its own kind of reasoning*, necessarily incorrect. Either there *is* such a thing as a mind-independent reality and materialistic science can never address it all, or there *isn't*, in which case the premise of scientific materialism — which posits the 'reality' of a universe independent of all experience — cannot stand.

This 'either/or', however, is itself a component of precisely the niche-reasoning that materialistic science employs. In logic, it is known as the 'Law of Excluded Middle', which says that either a proposition is true or its negation must be. We have seen of how little use this law is in certain instances when we considered the statement 'The beech tree is there'. If a statement is incoherent, neither it *nor* its negation ('The beech tree is not there') can be meaningfully said to be true or false. The Law of Excluded Middle does not apply.

In fact, however, the Second Parable does not *have* to assume the 'existence' of unexperienced 'things'. This assumption, employed by scientific materialism, *entails* the conclusion of the Second Parable that there is a 'beyond', that our knowledge of the universe *cannot* be complete. Without the assumption, though, we still remain in a realm in which the Second Parable can apply. We are left, namely, in the realm of experience. Even if we do not claim to make sense of the unexperienced beech tree, we can still take a lesson from the Second Parable: that there can always be a 'beyond'—not, in this case, past propositions about how things are, but past my *experience*—as there is a 'beyond' (namely the visual aspects of the beech tree) past the experience of the blind.

And who can say whether or how or when or where the line between experience and what is currently beyond experience may be capable of being breached? Who can say whether that which is currently beyond experience can turn into actual experience, as when the blind person begins to see? And if this breach occurs, who can say what lies beyond and to what kind of experience it is accessible? And when this breach occurs, the Second Parable is not finished—we merely have a new border to our experience, a new 'beyond', as when the formerly blind person who now sees realises that yet another 'sense' would 'know' the beech tree in yet another light. The Second Parable is never finished; it is an envelope that, when opened, reveals yet another envelope.

The First and Second Parables, in this reading, complement rather than contradict each other. The First says, I cannot make sense of the idea of a beech tree existing in the absence of any experience. The Second says, even the experienced beech tree has more to it and always will. Both point directly to mysteries, mysteries that evade the niche-reason so effectively employed for practical purposes by our sciences.

Error and Loss

There are two kinds of mysteries. The first kind represents something that we do not know but could. *Someone* murdered Roger Ackeroyd. We don't know who, so we call it a mystery. But Hercule Poirot finds out and the mystery is solved.

The second kind is an enduring mystery. It is something that *can't* be figured out and answered with a proposition. There is no answer. There is not even a question. It is not a 'Whodunnit'? It is the beech tree.

When we reach our limits, the limits of our niche-reason, we have reached the limits of propositional thinking. But this does not mean we stop. Animals never even engage in propositional thinking. After the limits of propositional thinking have been reached and *recognised*, we can no longer form coherent statements. We are left, instead, with non-propositional experience. We are left with the animals.

We are rarely left so. We are mostly addicted to our propositions. We believe in them. When we are shopping, we believe that we are shopping. When we go to bed, we go to bed. When we go for a hike, we go for a hike. We speak of our 'selves' as 'having' experiences, as if the self and the experience were two different entities. We speak of 'things' as if it were coherent for them to 'exist' outside of all experience. Our niche-reason gives us propositions and we follow them. Surely, they are useful. Surely, on one level, they comfort us. Who of us could *handle* living without them, even for a short time? Who could handle being a wolf?

And yet they limit us. They filter our experience, both in that they reduce what we actually perceive to that which we have learned is relevant to the situation in which we find ourselves (we are human beings, we are shopping now, objects have permanence) and because they limit what is available to our thought. This is practically useful, but also leaves us diminished. Recognising this—recognising, via the Parables, that our most basic propositions, while useful, are themselves ontological and thus incoherent; *placing* the propositions where they belong and believing they belong there—can allow for an extension of experience and, as I will argue shortly, of 'truth'.

Scientific materialism does us its greatest disservice by suggesting that there are no mysteries, by suggesting that we know the answers to the ultimate questions and that these answers are propositions. This view is incoherent on so many levels that it is a wonder it has been put over on us. Not only does scientific materialism in fact not answer the ultimate propositional question of why there is something instead of nothing; it cannot even deal in a coherent form with the relationship between *experience* and *what is experienced*. Its claim of a neutral, mind-independent, indifferent universe to which experience is a superfluous, random add-on cannot be squared with the reliance of the very meaning of the word 'existence' on experience, while its suggestion that the repeatable, measurable, objective objects of scientific study form the entirety of what 'exists' is the narrowest of tunnel visions. The tragedy is that it has convinced so many of us that our effective niche-thinking can answer, or even coherently pose, questions of a completely different sort from those for which it was designed, and that it has answered, or will answer, these questions, leaving us in a thoroughly-known world devoid of mystery. We are to pull up our socks and courageously face this bleak, thoroughly-known existence.

My view not only denies the coherence of the propositional 'truth' scientific materialism delivers; it also suggests that our search for truth and meaning *cannot be propositional*. It has been shunted onto this track by the overvaluation of niche-reasoning,

Error and Loss

and this from before Plato's time onward. Our real search for truth and meaning, I would suggest, cannot but be *experiential*. To satisfy it, rather than reasoning towards ultimate propositions with a language that is incapable of doing this coherently, we need to experience as deeply, richly, fully as we can. We need to lay ourselves *open* to new perceptions (Second Parable, Part Two), conceptions, languages, *non*-languages, beings. Our fellow animal species give us many, many examples of openings, broadenings, deepenings of perception, of experience. Reports from fellow human beings who have transcended the confines of conventional experience should also give us warrant to believe that, if we tune our attention, if we tune especially our *openness* to this task, we may experience non-propositional truths, mysteries and 'realities' not dreamt of in our philosophy.

Of course, the idea that we need to seek our 'truth' in experience rather than in propositions is hardly new. Romanticism, spiritual traditions, a host of self-help techniques and much else all point in this direction. What I believe to be essential, and the reason for writing this book, is *against what background* does one extend, deepen, open one's experience? If against the background of scientific materialism, one is seeking a 'truth' which is of one's own creating; one's deep, transcendent experience is ultimately explainable by the interaction of matter; this interaction creates the subjective experience of transcendence as the reaction of sodium and chlorine produces table salt. It is unwarranted to speak of being in touch with a 'beyond', a mystery. The universe is still indifferent and neutral and there is no 'beyond' outside of one's feeling of a 'beyond'. The transcendence is explained and grounded. I could create this transcendent feeling at will and will be able to do so in the future, by stimulating the appropriate parts of a material human brain as happens, for example, when one ingests psilocybin or brings about a self-induced vision by training in a meditative or contemplative tradition. There is a *feeling* of transcendence, but no 'beyond', no mystery, to which it transcends.

It is one thing to have a transcendent experience against this background and another to have the same experience against the background that I have argued for in this book. That background is mystery. This is not a propositional statement—it is the opposite of one, mystery being the absence of a covering proposition. It says merely, we are here, we stand here, we don't know. The world-view that defines what exists as ultimately reducible to nothing but matter in motion is incoherent, but neither is there a 'replacement' world-view that defines it as something else, because propositional world-views are all illusions of a language and reason that are not made for such stuff. We are left with an experience that is to be 'taken seriously'—not as the basis for yet another propositional world-view, but as part of a *lived* world-view, a *way of being*. We are left with a licence to enchantment. It does not describe or prescribe the enchantment, but rather rids us of the illusion that forbids it.

Error and Loss

If a lion could speak, we could not understand him.
— Wittgenstein

I have maintained in this book that the saturation of our lives with advanced technology contributes to a generally watered-down experience. By watered-down, I mean absent the stance of wonder-awe-terror towards actual phenomena, and hence also absent a certain intensity of experience which arises when one is confronted with phenomena that harbour mystery. The technology that saturates our lives seems to serve as a constant reminder that we have explanations for everything. These explanations are based on a materialistic science. Both implicitly with a technology that demonstrates our mastery and explicitly in the reigning philosophical orthodoxy in the academy, a world-view has developed that I refer to as scientific materialism. This is different from materialistic science but related to it. Materialistic science currently explains and predicts selected phenomena fundamentally by reference to a model in which physical matter is subject to force fields but makes no philosophical claims about the 'reality' or 'completeness' of this model. Scientific materialism, on the other hand, claims that matter and force fields are the ultimate reality and everything can be explained and predicted in terms that ultimately (gradually, hierarchically) can be reduced to them.

I have argued that while the success of science and the saturation of our lives with advanced technology might *seem* to warrant a philosophy of scientific materialism, this 'seeming' is an illusion. In fact, materialistic science itself argues *against* scientific materialism as a world-view. A materialistic science suggests that we who formulate world-views are the products of a blind algorithm which selects for reproductive advantage, and that while it is to be expected that a species, *Homo sapiens*, whose evolutionary niche is the ability to strategise, invent and control nature, would be *good* at doing exactly that and would have developed abilities, in this case cognitive and linguistic, effective at strategising, inventing and controlling nature, it would *not* predict that this species would be good at discovering what is ultimately true about the cosmos. We ought to be good at building Airbuses and smart phones, but not at developing a metaphysics. I have argued that the very cognitive abilities that promote effective strategising, inventing and control of nature in fact *hinder Homo sapiens* in its attempt to achieve the latter goal. An incoherent but effective belief in the permanence of objects, a tendency to believe in the possible reality of counterfactuals, an abstracting of space (maps) and time (clocks and calendars) from lived experience, the invention of a 'self' mediating between two separated worlds, a belief in causality behind correlation all contribute to mastery of the niche, but all are incoherent descriptions of 'reality'. Yet poor *Homo sapiens* is in a bind, because the kind of mind that is good at solving practical problems naturally *wants* to answer the bigger questions as well.

Error and Loss

The problem is that the bigger questions are being asked in the same terms as the practical ones, and the same cognitive tools are used to attack them, when in fact the bigger questions cannot even be coherently formulated in these borrowed terms. There are no questions that make sense and thus there are no answers.

There is an overpowering temptation to think that if a materialistic science gets so much *right*, it must somehow be the basis for a coherent world-view. This argument, however, fails to take into account the extremely *selective* questions that the materialistic science *confines itself* to posing..

Scientific materialism thus abuses materialistic science on several counts. It not only attempts to use the tools designed for one purpose (strategising, inventing, control) for a completely different purpose (discovering a proposition about ultimate reality); it also attempts to inflate the success record of materialistic science to include all of 'reality' rather than the selected phenomena that materialistic science limits itself to. Furthermore, it makes claims for the cognitive abilities of *Homo sapiens* that are inconsistent with materialistic science's own predictions concerning the species.

If my argument is accepted, it only remains to ask where this leaves us. What does it mean to live with a useful, selective, materialistic science *without* a philosophy of scientific materialism behind it?

I would like to look at three examples which might help us to work this out. The first example is that of the phenomenon of sound. By asking its selective questions of this phenomenon (as in the Third Parable), materialistic science arrives at a version of sound, equally accessible to deaf and hearing persons, according to which sound is a series of longitudinal compressions and rarefactions in a medium. (Beethoven, who asked quite different questions of sound, questions not expressible in our niche-language, came up, of course, with quite different answers—answers which rendered it tragic when he actually did become deaf.) The materialistic version of sound is useful for many purposes, such as the making of iPods, on which the hearing among us can listen to Beethoven's music. It is in no way, however, a complete or even a good description of the phenomenon of sound. I would claim that the best, most complete description of the phenomenon of sound is to be had by *experiencing a sound*, by *hearing*. It is for this reason that the hearing know what sound is, while the deaf, except via an extremely belaboured twisting of ideas, do not. Rarefactions and compressions in a medium present a model which allows one to control and manipulate sound but can hardly be said to be the 'reality' of sound. The 'sound' of materialistic science (which a great number of people would say is what sound 'really' is) is a poor creature indeed compared to what it is to *hear a sound*.

The second example is the phenomenon of consciousness. By asking its selective questions of consciousness, materialistic science arrives at a version of consciousness according to which consciousness is reduced (after a gradual descent through vast and complex hierarchies of organisation) to a brain state. Just as certain longitudinal compressions and rarefactions in a medium produce a given sound (say, a 440 Hz A of 70 decibels), so does a certain physical brain state produce a certain quality of consciousness (say, a sense of grief or the image of a beech tree). Again, this is useful for many purposes including diagnosing and treating mental diseases, but as a description of 'consciousness' a physical brain state, with however many layers of complexities one may draw out of it, is, if possible, an even more paltry thing than a description of sound as compressions in a medium. Materialistic science has again *selected* that part of the phenomenon in question with which

Error and Loss

it can deal and has produced a *useful*, but far from complete or even adequate, description of the phenomenon. The best, most complete description of the phenomenon 'consciousness' is to be had by *being conscious*.

My third example is the phenomenon of lightning. In the same way as with sound and consciousness, materialistic science asks its selective questions of the phenomenon of lightning and describes it as the balancing out of a voltage difference by the movement of electrons from one location to another, a movement allowed for an instant by the ionisation of a pathway of air—which, on deionising, releases vast amounts of electromagnetic radiation one of whose effects is to create a series of compressions and rarefactions in the air.

This description, again, does its job. One could objectively and repeatedly measure aspects of the occurrence, most easily with artificially produced lightning in a lab. Is it, however, a good or complete description of lightning? It could be understood by a student of physics who has never experienced lightning. In what sense, though, would such a student know what lightning is? Just as with sound or consciousness, the materialist scientific description of lightning *leaves out the lightning*. The best, most complete description of lightning is to be had by experiencing a lightning storm. (And the more one is capable of *opening oneself* to the storm, the better and more complete the 'description'.)

In these three examples we notice a *reversal* of the dogma that many of us have been unconsciously or consciously living by all our lives, the dogma of scientific materialism. This dogma states that the *underlying reality*, the *most explicit description* of the phenomenon in question, is that of our materialistic science. Our experience is *just* subjective, illusory, *optional*—what is *really* happening is what our materialistic science has selected *from* the experience. Having shown this dogma to be both incoherent *and* contrary to what materialistic science itself would have us expect, we have turned the affair on its head. I believe that it is *obvious* from the examples above that the *most fundamental description of the phenomenon is the experience*, not the elements selected from it for use in the scientific model. If we want to know how the universe *is* in any meaningful sense, we must not seek it in propositions, but in *lived experience*. Scientific materialism has the pernicious effect of diminishing lived experience by *devaluing* its truth in favour of propositions that turn out to be *incoherent*.

Another look at animals will bring this idea home, and in two different ways. First, animals experience the world radically differently from us. Their experience — which, since they neither select for objective, measurable and repeatable phenomena nor make ontological propositions, is the *only* candidate for their 'reality' — is probably impossible (famously, the bat) to imagine, but we can at least make a stab at conceiving of a reality that is not, like ours, self-conscious, threaded with counterfactuals, causes, maps and clocks — perhaps we ourselves, in certain exceptional moments, also know something close to the purity of animal experience. These animal realities are all around us and we tend to devalue them as 'truths' because we have come to see truth as propositional and because we are the only beings capable of formulating propositions. If we begin to see truth as experiential, however, we might become somewhat more humble and admit the validity of animal experience as equal to our own; indeed, the truth of animal experience might seem superior to ours in our times of endless wrestling with 'what-ifs' and regrets, our confusions about what means what to us. A materialistic science, indeed, assigns us no priority over the animals, and it is curious (or perhaps not so) that scientific materialism privileges

100

our perspective to such an extent that propositions seem to be the measure of truth, propositions that, handily, only we are equipped to make.

Second, the amazing capacities of animals, in so many respects superior to our own — more acute senses (wolves' sense of smell, the vision of birds of prey), almost or completely 'other' senses (bats' echolocation, vipers' infrared vision, the pinpoint long-distance navigational sense of birds and fish), untutored behaviour (birthing, mothering, self-defence) — point out that our experience is parochial and that *experience* can take on fantastical, unimaginable forms. To me this holds out a concrete hope that our experience can be *expanded*, that the experience of our 'reality' is not bounded by what have come to be conventional human expectations. I mean this in the sense of the Second Parable of the Beech Tree: that if our search for truth is experiential rather than propositional, we have every reason to believe that our experience is capable of ever more dimensions made possible either by developing our commonly-held senses, perceptions, languages past their current limits (the extreme sensitivity of the blind to nonvisual cues in their environment suggests a model) or even by developing perceptions which are not conventionally deemed 'ordinary'. A vast range of non-ordinary experiences has been reported (and generally ignored, thanks to scientific materialism) by our fellow human beings, experiences sometimes occurring spontaneously and sometimes as a result of traditions of contemplation, meditation, yoga, shamanism, ingesting hallucinogenic plants, etc. Dreams represent a variety of non-ordinary experience accessible to almost everyone. Extended immersion in the natural world away from civilisation, as I have mentioned, personally gives me such experience.

This is not a call to rush out to every New Age boutique that opens its doors. New Age business is full of shams and superficialities. It is a call, however, to judge non-ordinary experiences on their own merits—are they a bunch of coiffured fluff (and not terribly non-ordinary after all) or do they bring a genuine enlargement of experience and thus of one's 'reality'?

Poetry, music, painting and the other arts also serve as portals into non-ordinary 'reality', and in our age it is not just the yogi or the seer but predominantly the artist who is celebrated as being in contact with this realm. Great art changes and enlarges the experience of the sensitive viewer. According to the ideas presented in this book, art does more than bring about pleasing or puzzling or exciting brain states; it may give us access to an experience which partakes of a mystery that is not reducible, ultimately, to the objective, repeatable and measurable, to the interactions of tiny particles. [19]

In Chapter 2, I listed four conventional objections to scientific materialism and suggested that, while cogent, they were of little effect because they shared the hidden assumption of scientific materialism itself. Let me close by spelling out that assumption and indicating why I believe that an awareness of it can break the hegemony of scientific materialism as a default world-view. The assumption—the 'Error' in this book's title—is that our niche-reasoning instinct is generally valid, valid beyond what our materialistic science in its neo-Darwinian form expects of it. From this follows naturally the entrenched belief that our reason is not only coherent but can claim completeness in its posing and handling of questions about what we call existence and reality. The

---

19   This is not to say that scientific materialists do not appreciate fine art. The question, as above with transcendent experiences, is, against what background? Is beauty, e.g., completely captured by identifying it as a particular type of feeling induced by a brain state? Or is there perhaps more to it, an unknowable, mysterious 'more'?

First Parable of the Beech Tree dealt with coherence, the Second and Third with completeness.

We have seen, however, that demolishing scientific materialism inflicts heavy collateral damage, for what has been demolished is not only scientific materialism but the possibility of *any* coherent and complete propositional world-view at all. It is only by going this deep, I believe, that one can break the stranglehold of our technology-saturated surroundings on our default world-view.

What opens up, then, is a new way of conceiving of a world-view, not as propositional, but as a way of being. With this conception it becomes meaningful to talk about the world-views of animals as well as of human beings. And the search for 'truth', for what is 'real', becomes not a hunt for the correct proposition but an openness to broader experience, to a 'knowing' analogous to the 'knowing' of the wolf, the bat, the viper. What are the limits of such 'knowing'? According to this view, these will not be determined in the academy or the laboratory, but are stretched and tested by every creature who walks in openness about the earth.

Acknowledgements

For their generous support of the project of writing this book I would like to thank Daniel Romualdez, Jessica Marshall and Peter Belhumeur, Jessie Griffiths, Remo Hertig and Becky Sinkler, along with the many others who contributed to the Indiegogo campaign that made it possible. Special thanks for reading or listening and providing feedback go to Jessica Marshall and Joshua, Sonia, and John Curtis. I am grateful to Giulio Mazzoli for helping me find my way through the zoo of particle physics. And I am especially grateful to Sam Bagg for his enthusiastic interest and support, for providing me with background reading and for a detailed response to the first draft which pushed me to take my ideas further than I had previously dared.

Error and Loss

CPSIA information can be obtained
at www.ICGtesting.com
Printed in the USA
BVHW08*0318310818
526144BV00003B/13/P